KU-734-693

Masterpieces
of European Painting
in the
National Gallery
London

Published by order of the Trustees
Publications Department
National Gallery
London

© THE NATIONAL GALLERY 1965

First published in November 1965

Printed in England by

TILLOTSONS (BOLTON) LIMITED

Bolton and London

Contents

Foreword

The fifty masterpieces reproduced in this book have been selected for a variety of reasons. In some cases good colour prints of important and popular pictures already existed; these have been used here, but in addition many new blocks have been specially made for this volume, of pictures whose suitability for reproduction in colour equalled their other claims for inclusion.

Any fifty pictures selected out of the Gallery's two thousand must inevitably omit some favourites – and some favourite painters. A completely personal anthology would be amusing to assemble but would probably prove more restricted in scope. The present selection ranges widely over the Gallery's very representative collection of all the European Schools of Painting; it opens in the fourteenth century with Italian pictures like *The Maries at the Sepulchre* (pl. 1) and closes with pictures painted well into the twentieth century, like Monet's *Water-lilies* (pl. 50). The result is not only a series of masterpieces over the centuries but an indication of the particular strengths and riches of the collection.

The National Gallery is unusual, if not unique, among the great European galleries in having been from its foundation intended as a public collection. It was founded in 1824 when Parliament purchased the collection of John Julius Angerstein (who had died the previous year) and also his house in Pall Mall which became the National Gallery for the first ten years of its existence. In 1838 the move was made to the present building in Trafalgar Square, then newly constructed on the designs of William Wilkins. It has since often been altered and enlarged, though the façade and dome remain as Wilkins designed them. At the time of writing, new plans for further extensions at the back of the buildings have been drawn up, necessitated by the increasing growth of the collection.

It is one of the most important aspects of a national collection that it should grow, responding to some extent to the development of public and private taste. The Gallery has been evolving in this way from the beginning. At first there was little eagerness among the Trustees to do more than acquire pictures by the most respected old masters, judged by a somewhat old-fashioned standard. Corporate bodies and committees are always liable to make conservative judgements. And it is significant that the most distinguished years of acquisition during the nineteenth century occurred when the final purchasing decision rested with the Director alone.

A thread of the Gallery's evolution can be traced through the pictures reproduced here. Probably every great English private collection in the early years of the nineteenth century possessed at least one Claude; Angerstein owned a particularly fine group, including the *Landscape with Cephalus and Procris* (pl. 32) which was thus among the nucleus of the National Collection. A moving spirit behind the concept of such a Collection for England had been another collector, Sir George Beaumont, who generously offered his pictures to the nation in 1823 on condition that a public gallery was built. He died in 1827, having deposited his pictures, which included inevitably work by Claude, but also by Rembrandt and Canaletto, and the magnificent *Château de Steen* (pl. 26) by Rubens. In the years that followed several splendid acquisitions were made, among them Poussin's *Bacchanalian Revel* (pl. 29), Titian's *Bacchus and Ariadne* (pl. 21) and Murillo's *Two Trinities* (pl. 33). The Gallery's sole Caravaggio, *The Supper at Emmaus* (pl. 25) was, significantly, a bequest not a purchase – a very fortunate one at a period when his great importance was little recognized. In 1831 the Gallery benefited from the bequest of the Rev. W. Holwell Carr, whose pictures included *S. George and the Dragon* (pl. 23) by Tintoretto, a painter equally little esteemed at the period and still under-represented in the collection. On Constable's death in 1837 a body of subscribers presented his *Cornfield* (pl. 45), one of the first 'modern' pictures to enter the Gallery. And these random but remarkable early years closed in 1842 with the purchase of the unique Jan van Eyck *Arnolfini Portrait* (pl. 4).

In the following year Charles Lock Eastlake became Keeper. He was to resign in 1847 but return triumphantly as Director in 1855, equipped with full purchasing powers. During his keepership the Trustees acquired such outstanding works as Bellini's *Doge Loredan* (pl. 14), the first of its many pictures by Bellini, and Rubens's *Judgment of Paris* (pl. 27). Conscious less of superior minds than of supposedly superior station, the Trustees sometimes did not deign to take Eastlake's expert advice; to his successor as Keeper they appear to have seldom spoken. The dangers of amateur gentlemen are revealed by the history of the *Madonna and Child with S. John and Angels* (pl. 20), then as now considered a possible Michelangelo. Eastlake thought it in fact by Ghirlandaio, but he urged it on the Trustees in 1844, believing it obtainable at about £250. The owner refused this but the Trustees declined to negotiate further, owing to an adverse opinion expressed by the President of the Royal Academy. It was finally bought in 1870 after Eastlake's death, when the Trustees paid £2,000.

Between Eastlake's resignation as Keeper and his return in 1855, the Gallery went through a period of very considerable criticism, in part coinciding with the legal tangle over Turner's bequest of his own work to the nation. Eventually a settlement was reached and in 1856, along with other paintings by him, the *Ulysses deriding Polyphemus* (pl. 43) and *Steamer in a Snowstorm* (pl. 44) became part of the Collection. In 1853 a Select Committee had been appointed by the House of Commons to enquire into all the Gallery's affairs and its policy (or lack of policy) in purchasing. As a result of this, Eastlake, who had become President of the Royal Academy, became also Director, and the policy was established that pictures should be acquired which were not only beautiful works of art but which would serve in 'instructing the public in the history of art'.

Eastlake combined the gifts of connoisseur and public servant. He remained an active and inspired Director until his death at Pisa on Christmas Day, 1865. During the ten-year period of his reign, many of the Gallery's most familiar masterpieces were acquired and its character was largely fixed. Among early Italian pictures Eastlake obtained the large Pollaiuolo *Martyrdom of S. Sebastian* (pl. 9), Bellini's *Madonna of the Meadow* (pl. 13), Botticelli's *Portrait of a Young Man* (pl. 10). He bought the *Baptism of Christ* (pl. 8) by Piero della Francesca for £241 in 1861, and that year presented to the Gallery Filippo Lippi's *Annunciation* (pl. 7). Other schools were not neglected; Ruisdael's *Waterfall* (pl. 35) and Reynolds's *Captain Orme* (pl. 39) were both acquired during his directorship, as was Sarto's *Portrait of a Young Man* (pl. 16). The impetus continued after East-lake's death, with the current turning away from Italy from which so much had been drawn. In 1871 the collection of Dutch and Flemish pictures formed by Sir Robert Peel was purchased from his son; the two outstanding works were Rubens's *Chapeau de Paille* (pl. 28) and Hobbema's *Avenue* (pl. 36). Before the end of the century there had been added the Velazquez full-length of *Philip IV* (pl. 30), Holbein's *Ambassadors* (pl. 18) and Vermeer's *Lady at the Virginals* (pl. 34). But by the end of the century – in fact, in 1894 – the Director's power as buyer had vanished, along with the opportunities, it might seem, to acquire masterpieces for the nation. Sometimes it was initiative rather than opportunity which was lacking. No sooner had the Trustees acquired the full power of purchasing than they exercised it by declining to pursue the matter of acquiring Lord Darnley's superb Titian *Rape of Europa* which thereupon went to America.

There were still generous bequests. One of the largest was that of George Salting in 1920 which included the rare masterpiece of the *Virgin and Child* (pl. 3) by Campin. Important single acquisitions were made in the years between the two world wars when Bruegel's *Adoration of the Magi* (pl. 19) and Titian's *Vendramin Family* (pl. 22) and Ingres' *Madame Moitessier* (pl. 46) were purchased, the Titian with the aid of a large Exchequer grant. In recent years Government and, where forthcoming, private aid has increasingly had to be sought to enable the Gallery to acquire great paintings in a highly competitive world of rapidly rising picture prices and the shrinking number of available masterpieces. Nowadays no school of painting is out of fashion, though the Italian fifteenth century seems, paradoxically, somewhat neglected, while French nineteenth century pictures are being esteemed perhaps beyond their merits – the inevitable result of a time-lag in appreciation.

The Gallery can hardly plan a systematic policy of acquisition where so much depends upon availability at any moment: availability of a picture seldom coinciding with availability of funds. It has concentrated on those two aspects of policy laid down more than a hundred years ago, combining the task of illustrating the history of art with acquisition of great works of art. In 1954 it was possible to acquire the wonderful late Gainsborough portrait, *The Morning Walk* (pl. 40), which came with help from the National Art-Collections Fund – only one example of a master-piece saved for the country by that body's effort. The most famous instance will perhaps always be the unprecedented efforts that eventually succeeded in obtaining for the nation Leonardo da Vinci's cartoon of the *Madonna and Child with SS. Anne and John the Baptist* (cover) which was acquired in 1962 after a public subscription had been raised by the National Art-Collections Fund to acquire it from the Royal Academy. To achieve this, large contributions were made by the Fund itself, the Pilgrim Trust, the Gallery's Annual Grant and a Special Exchequer Grant. It was presented by the National Art-Collections Fund and now hangs by itself in a special room at the Gallery.

By the terms of the Finance Act in 1956 the Chancellor of the Exchequer was allowed to accept outstanding works of art in lieu of payment of estate duty. Several masterpieces have thus entered the collection, among them Memlinc's *Donne Triptych* (pl. 12) which takes its place amid the Gallery's splendid array of Netherlandish pictures, built up discriminatingly from the first. For long, little attention was paid to the neighbouring German School, though part of a collection of early German pictures was bought in 1854 and some others were presented by Queen Victoria in memory of the Prince Consort. In very recent years two notable German pictures have been bought: Cranach's sophisticated mythology of *Cupid complaining to Venus* (pl. 17) and a very rare *Landscape* (pl. 15) by Altdorfer – one of the only two known pure landscape pictures by this most important and attractive of German painters.

These pictures were acquired in their own right and also with the awareness of how under-represented the German School was in the Collection. More serious have been the deficiencies in the French School of the eighteenth and nineteenth centuries. It remains a grave lack that there is still little to convey the achievements of French rococo or neo-classic painting (no fine Boucher, and no David at all). The first painting by Delacroix was bought at the Degas sale in 1918: the impressive but not truly typical *Baron Schwiter* (pl. 47). In the previous year the bequest of Sir Hugh Lane had brought the Gallery a group of French nineteenth century pictures which contained its first pictures by Renoir and Manet, including *La Musique aux Tuileries* (pl. 48). But the achievements of the Impressionists and the leading painters who followed them have until very recently indeed not been represented on a worthy scale. Great efforts have been made, culminating in the purchase of two large-size and quintessential canvases which happen to represent two distinct types of vision, the logical outcome of nineteenth century artistic development but relevant too for developments in our own century: Monet's very late *Water-lilies* (pl. 50) and Cézanne's *Grandes Baigneuses* (pl. 49). The latter was finally acquired, after prolonged and anxious negotiation, in 1964, with the help of a considerable Exchequer grant and an outstandingly munificent contribution from the Max Rayne Foundation.

As well as the history of painting, there is always the history of the collecting of pictures and this too has its fascination, because the ultimate criterion is not cash but taste. The fifty masterpieces in this book, reproduced in approximately chronological order, can thus be mentally re-assembled to reveal something of the course of collecting pictures for the nation over a period little short of a century and a half.

September, 1965

MASTERPIECES OF EUROPEAN PAINTING
IN THE NATIONAL GALLERY, LONDON

ORCAGNA

(Active *ca.* 1343; died 1368/9)

His real name was ANDREA DI CIONE; Orcagna appears to be a corruption of Arcangelo. He was active at Florence not only as a painter but as sculptor and architect, and was the leading painter of his day in Florence. His only certain painting is the large altarpiece in the Strozzi Chapel of S. Maria Novella (which is signed and dated 1357). He had two brothers, Nardo and Jacopo, who were also active as painters. There is a large body of work which is Orcagnesque in style and which has not yet been satisfactorily attributed.

The Gallery owns a group of pictures in the style of Orcagna which are the principal remains of the high altarpiece of S. Pier Maggiore at Florence, and the present picture is one panel from this. In addition, there are several other Orcagnesque paintings in the collection.

THE MARIES AT THE SEPULCHRE

The painter of this picture is not certainly known, but it can hardly have been Orcagna himself who was dead at the time the altarpiece in S. Pier Maggiore was planned. It must be seen as a reflection of his popular style and as a minor masterpiece, controlled by Orcagna's conventions and lyrically clear in its story telling – as vivid as the simple words of some carol. Between the giant figures of Giotto (died in 1337) and Masaccio (born in 1401), Florentine painting turned away from preoccupations with three-dimensional space, volume and perspective. Orcagna, despite his activity as a sculptor, had other interests. He announces the typically Florentine interest in linear effects which culminates at the end of the fifteenth century with Botticelli. In this scene of the Maries arriving to find Christ risen and the angels about the empty sepulchre, there is hardly more attempt at drama than at realising space in depth. A gold sky sharply delimits the area, with the formal rocky landscape and few trees. Against this screen the Maries stand, immobile, but gazing with nearly witch-like intensity, each clasping her jar of ointment, at the bland angel seated on the tomb. Nothing distracts from the silent, significant encounter; the small areas of ornament – patterning of the simple robes, decoration on the tomb, the flower-studded grass – are subordinated to the sharp fretwork shapes which interlock across the single picture plane. The faces are either in full, or nearly full, profile, giving a keen air that is enhanced by the narrow eyes and straight lips. Something of the same intense concentration, even rigidity, is felt throughout the picture; and it is this which gives such conviction to it.

Panel, 37½ × 19½ (0·95 × 0·49). Bought with a selection of the Lombardi-Baldi collection, Florence, in 1857, along with the other parts of the S. Pier Maggiore altarpiece. They had been acquired by Francesco Lombardi and Ugo Baldi in 1846 from Marchese Pucci; he had inherited them from the della Rena family, to whose chapel at S. Pier Maggiore the pictures were removed after having been the high altarpiece.

MASACCIO

(1401-1427/9)

His proper name was TOMMASO DI GIOVANNI, but he was from early times called *Masaccio*. According to Vasari the nickname was given to him because of his carelessness in practical affairs. He was born at S. Giovanni Valdarno, near Florence; by 1422 he was living in Florence. In 1426 he was at Pisa and is known to have died at Rome. Some frescoes in the Brancacci Chapel of the Carmine at Florence represent his style at its finest. Inevitably in such a short career, there are few pictures. The only documented work by Masaccio is a polyptych painted for the Church of the Carmine at Pisa; he began the painting of this on 19 February 1426 and it was destined for a chapel that had been begun the previous year. The Gallery owns the central panel of this altarpiece (other portions of which are scattered throughout the world), which is the present picture.

THE VIRGIN AND CHILD

With Donatello and Brunelleschi, Masaccio makes up a trinity of the arts – of sculptor, architect and painter – which virtually created the Renaissance at Florence. Even if records did not reveal it, one might guess at Masaccio's friendship with these two men, and the *Virgin and Child* is full of a painter's response to their interests and their revolutionary art: with an intensely human, positively sculpted group of mother and child seated on a Brunelleschian throne. While Masaccio was engaged on the Carmine altarpiece, Donatello was actually in Pisa and it is tempting to think of them together looking at the sculpture of the Pisano there – some hints from which are perhaps present in Masaccio's picture. In a remarkable way it aims at a type of logically natural – and, as it were, accurate – art. The sheer bulk of bodies is conveyed, the Child a solid, naked figure cradled amid the modelled folds of the Virgin's robe, and the appearance of objects in space. Thus the Child's halo is shown foreshortened; the Virgin and Child group casts a shadow on the throne which is itself shaped to suggest solidity. The Virgin and Child are grave, even sad, presences. The Child puts a grape to his mouth in literal foretaste, perhaps, of the Passion against which his Mother cannot protect him. And in a panel above them the Crucifixion was shown.

The attendant angels are solemn-faced too, absorbed in their thin stringed music-making. The spectator does not stand amazed at the intricate splendour of the vision – as, for instance, in Tura's treatment of the theme (Pl. 11) – but is moved by these simply-coloured, monumental shapes which have an enduring sense of being eternal.

Panel, 53¼ × 28¾ (1·355 × 0·73). Bought in 1916 from Canon Sutton, with the aid of a contribution from the National Art-Collections Fund. He was the nephew of the Rev. F. H. Sutton who is stated to have owned the picture by 1864. Earlier in the collections of Samuel Woodburn and Miss Woodburn (in 1855). The altarpiece had probably left the Carmine Church by about 1635.

Robert CAMPIN

(1378/9-1444)

He is mentioned as a master painter at Tournai in 1406 but cannot have been born there since he did not become a citizen until 1410. Several paintings are reasonably attributed to him, although none is signed, dated, or documented. Some pictures are known by a pupil of his, Jacques Daret, and he had another pupil who is probably to be identified with the famous painter Rogier van der Weyden. Campin was certainly active contemporaneously with Jan van Eyck (q.v.) but his style is much more 'bourgeois' and even uncouth; he represents a reaction against the courtly elegance of the International Style, with new emphasis on realism.

The Gallery also owns two forceful portraits, of a man and woman, presumably husband and wife, which are ascribed to the same artist.

THE VIRGIN AND CHILD

No longer courtly or graceful, painting takes a new direction with Campin: towards realism. This difficult word luckily need not be defined here, for Campin's picture shows well enough one sense of it. Instead of those elaborate gilded and punched haloes which had decorated the heads of sacred persons in Gothic art, the Madonna here has a halo contrived out of the wickerwork firescreen; and she nurses the Child in a carefully observed fifteenth century Flemish interior. Although the Madonna's dress is ornamented with the unrealistic detail of a jewelled border the dress is shown with a perfectly realistic seam. Through the open window is seen a complete town in miniature with people going busily about their affairs (an urban activity in contrast to the country pursuits of the people in Bellini's *Madonna of the Meadow*, Pl. 13). Both pictures place the subject firmly in the life of their own country and time. It is still debated whether the 'realism' of Campin preceded that of Jan van Eyck, and Campin's identity as the painter of this picture and others similar in style is also vexed. Such questions may safely be left to scholars. But if, as seems very likely, this picture is by Campin – and possibly early work – then it is by a painter who was already practising at Tournai in 1406. There is not only a certain amount of revolution in the artist's attitude to his subject. The actual medium of oil paint is handled with new luminous dexterity, most apparent in the mauve-white dress of the Madonna.

Panel, 25 × 19¼ (0·635 × 0·49). Bequeathed by George Salting in 1910. It had been acquired by him in 1902, having previously been in the Somzée collection since 1875. Earlier in Italy and apparently in a collection at Parma.

Jan van EYCK

(Active 1422; died 1441)

Jan van Eyck was born perhaps at Maaseyck in present-day Belgium. Nothing is known of his early training or life; he is first recorded in the years 1422-4 when he was working at The Hague for Count John of Bavaria. From 1425 he served Duke Philip the Good of Burgundy, sometimes on diplomatic missions, and lived at Bruges where he died. His most famous work is the *Adoration of the Lamb* polyptych in the Cathedral at Ghent: this has an inscription recording it as begun by Hubrecht van Eyck who is presumed to be Jan's brother – but no pictures certainly by him exist.

As well as the present picture, the Gallery possesses two male portraits by Jan van Eyck (both signed and dated down to the exact day).

THE MARRIAGE OF GIOVANNI (?) ARNOLFINI AND GIOVANNA CENAMI (?)

Signed in legal-style lettering: *Johannes de eyck fuit hic. 1434*, this is perhaps the first double portrait in European painting. Its hieratic character emphasizes that it is more than a genre scene. There are indications that a marriage (or betrothal) ceremony is taking place; the unusual words of the signature suggest that van Eyck records himself there as a witness, and perhaps the picture was intended as a document of the ceremony. In pure genre it would be odd that one candle of the chandelier should be lit in broad daylight. The dog can be explained as a symbol of marital fidelity. Even the bedroom has been explained, though actually it was common for bedrooms to serve as reception and living rooms for people much grander than the pair here. The sitters have been cautiously identified: Giovanni Arnolfini was a merchant from Lucca living at Bruges who married Giovanna Cenami whose father was also from Lucca but lived in Paris. Their physiognomy does not suggest Italians, and despite the wonderfully observed detail of their bedroom they themselves seem to resist scrutiny. But the slightly chilly air the picture exudes cannot detract from van Eyck's ability to create an ordered spatial world. The eye travels down the room to the mirror reflecting back the sitters and also showing two figures entering at the door. And so the Arnolfini pair are painted fixed within an enclosed cube (the sixth side reflected in the mirror), almost in a dimension outside time.

Panel, 32¼ × 23½ (0·818 × 0·597); signed and dated 1434.   Bought from Major-General James Hay in 1842; he is stated to have acquired the picture at Brussels in 1815 and then brought it to England where its purchase was considered by the Prince Regent. Previously for long in Spain as part of the royal collection. It is first mentioned as owned by Don Diego de Guevara (who died in 1520). He gave it to Margaret of Austria, Regent of the Netherlands, from whom it passed to her great-niece the next Regent, Mary of Hungary, who left the Netherlands for Spain in 1556.

SASSETTA

(1392?–1450)

His real name was STEFANO DI GIOVANNI, but he is usually called Sassetta. He was perhaps born at Siena where he was active; there is evidence of his activity as a painter in 1423. There are several documented religious pictures and altarpieces. In 1437 he was commissioned to paint the high altarpiece for the church of S. Francesco at Sansepolcro, the birthplace of Piero della Francesca (q.v.), and he delivered it in 1444. Seven pictures from this altarpiece, which centred on the life of S. Francis of Assisi, are in the Gallery; the present panel is one of these.

THE LEGEND OF THE WOLF OF GUBBIO

S. Francis and the wolf are shown shaking hands outside the gate of the city of Gubbio, while at the left a notary takes down the details of the pact that has just been agreed. By this the wolf will stop eating the citizens—remains of some of whom can be seen strewn in the middle distance – and in return will be fed at public expense. Nothing seems to ripple the simple stream of Sassetta's belief in the story; he responds to it quite effortlessly and creates this perfect illustration of it. The artist's conviction in the power of art is perhaps what the picture suggests even more strongly. The convictions of art create a fresher world than any we – or Sassetta – know. Gubbio is reduced to the beautifully compact shape of the crenellated gateway, decorated too with the heads of the inquisitive, and timorous, female citizens. The landscape becomes this umber-coloured bare terrain broken only by the miniature trees, each plotted in its position as if on a chessboard, and the steeply curving path – whose curve is exultantly echoed by the birds wheeling in the cool blue sky above. The extent of Gubbio society, in age and rank, is symbolised by the group who witness the miracle. The whole scene is moving for its symbolic sense: with the beast's recognition of sanctity, followed by mankind's recognition of it too. And, of course, because the story of St. Francis of Assisi is an attractive legend rather different from the sheer facts about the lives of some other saints. The legend is full of harmony, response to nature, humanitarian appeal; and these are qualities which also characterise the art of Sassetta.

Panel, 34 × 20½ (0·865 × 0·52). Bought from Clarence Mackay, with the other six panels, in 1934, with contributions from the National Art-Collections Fund, Benjamin Guinness and Lord Bearsted. Previously in the collection of Clarence Mackay since 1927. The present picture had earlier belonged to the Comtesse de Féligonde who inherited it from the Comte de Martel. The group was sold in 1819 or later to a Florentine dealer by the Abate Angelucci of Arezzo who had received it from the Sigg. Sergiuliani. Cavalier Sergiuliani is stated to have bought the altarpiece from the friary of S. Francesco in about 1810.

AUSTRIAN SCHOOL, XV Century

There was a School of Painting in Austria especially active during the fifteenth century, with centres at Vienna and at Salzburg and elsewhere in that region. Most of the painters' names are not known or cannot be linked to surviving work. Their style evolved, with influences from the rest of Europe, and blended into an International Gothic idiom in the early part of the century. Its sources lie in illuminated manuscripts. It is distinguished by a softly flowing line and love of bright, heraldic colour; reality is treated in a courtly style in which the emphasis is laid on decorative effects. The Gallery owns a great masterpiece of this manner in the unique *Wilton Diptych*, presumably painted in England, but of which neither the authorship nor its exact nationality is known.

THE TRINITY WITH CHRIST CRUCIFIED

This picture is a rare object to find outside its country of origin (and it is almost as much as *objet d'art* as painting), especially in such good condition for its age. On all sides except the bottom it retains its original gold framing; and on the back of the panel a beautiful pattern of green leaves is painted on a white ground. The central panel of an altarpiece, painted probably about 1420, it shows a mystic vision of the Trinity in which God the Father is seated on the Throne of Mercy, holding up the Crucified Christ, and adored by angels. The subject makes for convenient stylisation, and the painter attempts only mildly three-dimensional effects, concentrating instead on a series of exquisite linear patterns, coloured in attractive greens and pinks, and set against the gold sky of heaven. It is a highly sophisticated art which has created the steep-pinnacled throne, flanked by the jagged scythes of the angels' wings, and the more gentle rhythm of the flowing folds of God the Father's robe, itself symmetrically spread out at the base of the throne. While his robe is plainly coloured, the angels wear dresses of almost Oriental splendour, embroidered with curling leaves and winged animals, which typify the International Gothic love of ornament. To some extent the picture represents a blend of two styles – Gothic modified by some awareness of new realistic interests – and is the product of a movement that could not be long prolonged. New artistic developments were soon to make it seem old-fashioned; but today its brilliant pattern-making and colour, like its distance from pictorial realism, make it easy to appreciate.

Panel, 46½ × 45¼ (1·181 × 1·15). Bought, with a donation from the National Art-Collections Fund, 1922. Earlier with various dealers in Germany, Italy and Switzerland.

Fra Filippo LIPPI

(*ca.* 1406?–1469)

He was an orphan who took his vows as a Carmelite monk at Florence in 1421; for about eleven years he remained at the Carmine in Florence, being mentioned as a painter early in 1431. He was much patronised by the Medici family. From 1452 he was working intermittently, not far from Florence, at Prato, where he painted an important fresco series. In 1467/9, he was working at Spoleto where he died. It was at Prato that he abducted a nun Lucrezia; by her he had a son Filippino who was also to become a famous painter. Filippo Lippi's style was founded on Masaccio (who had frescoed in the Brancacci chapel of the Carmine) but his later work shows a more graceful and lyrical approach.

The Gallery possesses three pictures by him, one of them a panel of *Seven Saints*, probably all connected with the Medici, and certainly painted as a pendant to the *Annunciation*.

THE ANNUNCIATION

It was probably the promised birth of a child to the Medici family which occasioned this picture. Along with its pair, *Seven Saints* (namesakes of members of the Medici), it comes from their palace at Florence; and their device of three feathers in a diamond ring is on the parapet which separates the angel from the Virgin in the picture here. The Medici patronised Fra Filippo a great deal and the *Annunciation* is typical of his best work. Not only are his paintings immediately attractive in colouring, but his particular blend of convention and naturalism, piety and profanity, naivety and intellectuality, results in an art that everyone can enjoy and no one dare despise. Of course he is far from the greatest Florentine in a century of great Florentine artists; he is not even the most competent, for in this picture the perspective of the parapet with its precariously balanced pot of lilies is haphazard and unconvincing. But the conventions of his century have somehow saved the painter both from sentiment and from insipidity; and the freshness of his imagination invests with immense charm this tranquil vision of the Virgin's loggia and dark cool garden where the peacock-winged angel comes so undramatically. There is no abrupt confrontation of natural and supernatural worlds: all is of a piece throughout, and even the hand of God piercing the cloud at the top of the picture seems unsurprising. The religious aspect of the scene is blended with the immediate circumstances of the commission. And the child about to be born to the Medici was quite possibly Lorenzo the Magnificent.

Panel, 27 × 60 (0·685 × 1·52). Presented by Sir Charles Eastlake in 1861 at the time the *Seven Saints* panel was purchased. Seen in 1855 by Eastlake in the shop of the Metzger Brothers at Florence; they had acquired both pictures shortly before 1848 from Palazzo Riccardi (Medici).

PIERO della Francesca

(Active 1439; died 1492)

He was a native of the small town of Sansepolcro in Tuscany, where he spent much of his life. He is first mentioned in 1439 when he was in Florence apparently as an assistant to Domenico Veneziano. In 1442 he was in Sansepolcro and he executed several works there, including the famous fresco of the *Resurrection*. He also worked in other places, among them Arezzo, where he frescoed the choir of S. Francesco with the story of the True Cross, and at Urbino, being much employed at the Court of Federigo da Montefeltro. He seems to have painted little after the 1470's, perhaps partly through increasing interest in perspective and mathematics and also through failing eyesight. During the last years of his life he appears to have been blind. Piero was virtually forgotten for more than three centuries after his death; though already rediscovered to some extent during the 19th century, it is only in the last fifty years that his greatness has been fully appreciated.

THE BAPTISM OF CHRIST

The Gallery was wise enough during the 19th century to acquire three pictures by Piero della Francesca: wise not only because of his genius but also because of the rarity of panel paintings by him. The *Baptism* was the first of these acquisitions, made in 1861 when he was still little known. It was painted, suitably enough, for the Priory of S. John the Baptist in Piero's home town of Sansepolcro, where it remained undisturbed for several centuries. Nothing perhaps could disturb it, for one's first and final sense of the picture is its timeless gravity. Water will flow forever from the bowl held up by the Baptist, and the shallow Jordan ripples palely about Christ's ankles, while the Dove hovers over the group in a sphere that seems outside time. There are no abrupt actions. At the left the angels are rooted like the tree, natural presences, witnesses that remain impassive; at the right the man taking off his shirt is held as if petrified, contained within the crystalline block of atmosphere that Piero creates about every object in his pictures. This sense of the eternal is not subjective. The proportions within the composition have all been carefully calculated and reveal Piero's interest in mathematics. Christ stands in the exact middle of the picture; a vertical line down its centre would bisect his body into two equal halves. An equilateral triangle is made from the point of the Baptist's upraised hand to the lower corners of the picture. The stripping man is approximately half the height of Christ; beyond, the figure in profile is again almost half his height. The result of these lucid intervals and proportions is a classical beauty that seems indestructible: a combination of passion and intellect which is typical of the Renaissance.

Panel, 66 × 45¾ (1·67 × 1·16). Bought at the Uzielli sale, London, 1861. Acquired on behalf of Matthew Uzielli by Sir J. C. Robinson in 1859 from the Bishop and Chapter of the Cathedral at Sansepolcro where the picture had been since suppression of the Priory of S. Giovanni Battista in 1808.

Antonio and Piero del POLLAIUOLO

(*ca.* 1432-1498; *ca.* 1441 – before 1496)

They were two brothers working in their native Florence and later at Rome, and they practised as sculptors as well as painters. The pictures known to be by Piero are not of such high standard as the *Martyrdom of S. Sebastian* and it seems likely that the two painters collaborated on it, and other works. It is their most famous and important surviving picture and was painted for the Oratory of S. Sebastiano in the Church of SS. Annunziata in Florence. It was commissioned by the Pucci family; two moors' heads on the building at the left in the picture are a reference to this family's coat-of-arms.

In addition to this very large picture, the Gallery owns a very small and beautiful panel of *Apollo and Daphne* which is by one or other – or both – Pollaiuolo.

THE MARTYRDOM OF S. SEBASTIAN

Other Florentine depictions of S. Sebastian are often devotional images of the saint standing pensively alone. Here the treatment is dynamic and exciting; though the saint remains passive, the bending and stretching archers form a ring of unleashed energy around him. Recent cleaning did little to establish whether the Pollaiuolo brothers worked jointly on this large altarpiece. It is early recorded as by Piero, but Vasari says it is by Antonio; whatever the answer, it remains a striking monument to new artistic ideas in Florence about 1475. Anatomy has become a pre-occupation which the subject offered good opportunities to express, while a sudden awareness of landscape results in the sweeping panorama of the Arno valley. Vasari says of Antonio that through dissecting corpses he understood the nude 'in a more modern way than the masters before him . . .' Science thus helps to dignify art, and in the same way the landscape is recorded with almost geological precision. The picture is an essay in the importance of the human body and the active sinewy archers become more admirable and attractive than the suffering martyr. But to first English appreciators of the Florentine Renaissance, even to Roscoe, such pictures, because of their realism, could be neither great nor elevated. This 'celebrated picture', Roscoe said, 'exhibits only a group of half-naked and vulgar wretches discharging their arrows at a miserable fellow-creature . . .' Painting, in his eyes, had to wait for the arrival of Michelangelo.

Panel, $114\frac{3}{4} \times 79\frac{3}{4}$ (2·915 × 2·025). Bought from Marchese Roberto Pucci at Florence in 1857. Probably it was removed about twenty years earlier to Palazzo Pucci from the Oratory for which it had been painted, where it is first recorded in 1510

Sandro BOTTICELLI

(*ca.* 1445-1510)

His full name was ALESSANDRO FILIPEPI. He may have been trained first as a goldsmith; there is an old tradition that as a painter he was trained by Fra Filippo Lippi (q.v.) and he seems also to have been influenced by the Pollaiuolo (q.v.). He created a personal style of extreme refinement, with emphasis on linear effects, which was to become out of date in his own lifetime. Little is known about his last years but he seems to have been affected by the doctrines of Savonarola and at that period probably painted only a few, deeply emotional, religious pictures. The obscurity of his reputation lasted for more than two centuries and he was not rediscovered as a major artist until the 19th century when the *Birth of Venus* and the *Primavera* (both in the Uffizi, Florence) gained their great fame.

The Gallery possessed several pictures by Botticelli, including the *Mystic Nativity* (signed and dated 1500).

PORTRAIT OF A YOUNG MAN

In this portrait Botticelli disdains effective setting or elaborate costume, and concentrates on the face alone. The costume indeed could hardly be simpler, and the sitter has no pretensions to rank or importance. The plain effect of the picture serves as a reminder of the comparatively simple world of fifteenth century republican Florence – still technically a republic, though virtually ruled by the Medici family. The plain dark background, along with the straightforward costume, serve all the more effectively to set off the sitter's face, seen in a pose of startling directness and brought into direct confrontation with the spectator's own. Although so vivid and personal, the features are yet schematised by the almost incised linear emphasis which cuts the shape of the lips, the curve of the eyelids and the singing, sinuous lines of the waving hair. Colour is subordinated throughout to line; and Botticelli's line is at once lyrical and strong, weaving the pattern that he wants and also managing at the same time to suggest sufficient volume.

The result is a portrait that gives almost the effect of being engraved. It is a portrait both realistic and idealistic: recognizably a Florentine youth of the period, but brother also to those angels who in other pictures by Botticelli press ardently about some group of the Madonna and Child.

Panel, 14¾ × 11⅛ (0·375 × 0·282). Bought at the Northwick Sale, 1857; previously recorded in the collection of Lord Northwick who had bought the picture at the Col. Matthew Smith Sale, London, in 1804.

Cosimo TURA

(shortly before 1431; died 1495)

He was the first important Ferrarese painter and perhaps the greatest of the group active there in the fifteenth century. In a document of 1431 he is mentioned as an infant; from 1451 he is recorded as active at Ferrara and he worked a good deal there for the court of the Este, the ruling family. He must have been influenced by Mantegna's work and also, in a less obvious way, by the frescoes painted at Ferrara by Piero della Francesca (q.v.). He was succeeded as court painter in 1486 and died poor.

The Gallery possesses four pictures by him which show the consistency of his highly personal and refined style; the most important of these pictures is the present altarpiece.

THE VIRGIN AND CHILD ENTHRONED

In fact, this is only the central panel from a large altarpiece of several compartments which was once in the monastery church of S. Giorgio fuori at Ferrara. It was commissioned by the Roverella family, probably in connection with the death of two of its members. One of them was shown on a wing of the altarpiece knocking for admission at the gate of heaven, and the central picture shows in effect Tura's vision of heaven. The Virgin and sleeping Child are placed on a throne which combines Old and New Testaments in the Hebrew lettering of the Commandments and, high up at the top, the symbols of the Four Evangelists. These are among the more patent symbols with which Tura surrounds his elegant group, accompanied by six angels providing a musical rhythm which has perhaps lulled the Child to sleep. Heaven is seen as a place of pink and green marble, carved into fantastic shapes, ornamented with grotesque faces and tiny winged figures of bronze. All the shapes, even those made by the clothes, are hard and petrified, beautifully clear in outline: patterned, folded, adorned, with curling tendrils of vine, suspended beads, wrought capitals. The Court of heaven is not so far away from the court of Ferrara. There is tremendous sophistication in this art, in which visual splendour is used to symbolise the celestial splendour of eternity. Although the Child sleeps unheeding, the Virgin is perhaps about to wake him. In another painting Tura has shown her with the sleeping Child – and also with a donor's prayer which may be echoed in the present picture: 'Awake thy Child, sweet mother, to fill my soul at last with happiness'.

Panel, 94¼ × 40 (2·39 × 1·02). Bought from Lady Eastlake in 1867, having previously belonged to Sir Charles Eastlake who obtained it from the Federico Frizzoni collection at Bergamo. The altarpiece had left S. Giorgio at a date not established, but it was *in situ* until 1709.

Hans MEMLINC

(Active 1465; died 1494)

Memlinc was German by birth, being born at Seligenstadt, near Frankfurt on the Main, but his active life was passed at Bruges. It is probable that he was trained in the Netherlands and his work shows the influence of Dirk Bouts and Rogier van der Weyden; he may even have been the latter's pupil. His calm religious pictures and often notably beautiful portraits do not really advance Flemish painting. To some extent he marks the end of a particular tradition and the eclipse of Bruges by the rising new centre of Antwerp.

The Gallery owns other pictures by Memlinc, but nothing as important as the present complete triptych.

THE DONNE TRIPTYCH

Sir John Donne and his wife Elizabeth, with their daughter, are introduced by SS. Catherine and Barbara to the enthroned Madonna and Child. Whether we are to imagine the donors already in heaven, or the Virgin and Child descended to earth, is a problem which probably never worried patron or painter of pictures like this. A particular interest of the altarpiece here, is that the donors are English and can be identified by the coats-of-arms on the pillars. Sir John Donne was a supporter of the Yorkist cause, knighted at Tewkesbury in 1471, and both he and his wife wear Yorkist collars of roses and suns, with Edward IV's pendant, the Lion of March. Unfortunately, nothing seems known about the picture's history before it appears in the eighteenth century. Memlinc is not the greatest of Flemish painters, but his carefully detailed placid world is enlivened by a gift for portraiture which places Sir John Donne beside the Gallery's Memlinc *Portrait of a Young Man at Prayer*. In both, the painter achieves an exquisitely controlled juxtaposition of black, red and white in the clothes of the sitters, an effect at once sensuous and austere; and he maps their faces with impassive candour. In the Donne triptych heaven and earth are one; there is little contrast between the donors and saints. The open loggia with its marble columns is invented architecture. The scene is set outside time, despite the contemporary landscape background, and has something of the cool perfection to be found again at a later date in Vermeer (Pl. 34).

Panel, centre 28 × 27 (0·71 × 0·68); wings 28 × 12 (0·71 × 0·30).
Acquired in 1957 from the Duke of Devonshire under the terms of the Finance Act, 1956. Previously in the Devonshire Collection for two centuries, passing into the collection in 1753 at the death of Lord Burlington. He was a lineal descendant of the donors shown in the picture, through their younger son Griffith.

Giovanni BELLINI

(Active *ca.* 1459; died 1516)

He was the son of the painter Jacopo Bellini and brother of another painter, Gentile; his sister married Andrea Mantegna. There is no certain date of birth for Giovanni Bellini who lived and worked throughout his career at Venice. He seems to have been employed by the Venetian State first in 1479. He painted important work, later destroyed by fire, in the Doge's Palace at Venice and became the outstanding painter and teacher of his generation there. A superb example of his official portrait work is the *Doge Leonardo Loredan* (Pl. 14 here) and the Gallery owns several fine examples of his treatment of a favourite theme, that of the Virgin and Child. Though there was probably some reciprocal influence, Bellini seems likely to have affected the style of both Giorgione (whom he outlived) and the young Titian (q.v.).

THE MADONNA OF THE MEADOW

After the urban Northern interior where Campin's Madonna and Child sit, Bellini's spacious countryside is as refreshing as cold air after an enclosed room. Comparison can hardly be just to Campin, for the beauty of Bellini's picture is communicated so immediately that one dismisses out of hand the less sensuous beauties of Campin. Bellini has too the advantage of Italian countryside in which to set his glowing group of Madonna and sleeping Child. Nobody before him had responded with such love to these stony fields where the white and dun oxen are tended by figures who might have wandered from Virgil's pastoral poems, and where as here a pale castle lifts its towers into pale liquid sky. The Madonna broods in prayer over the Child laid so starkly in her lap; and the daily life of the fields goes on unheeding. In another picture, late work like the picture here, Bellini again sets the Madonna in soft countryside — but there her Son lies dead across her knees and she extends her hands in grief. A note of muted poignancy is never far away in Bellini's best pictures, and this too recalls Virgil. But his supreme mastery is in use of light: it is light that here moulds the draperies of the Madonna and creates the luminous landscape beyond her. Bellini's discovery was to influence the whole Venetian school, and Titian supremely. He was an old man when Dürer met him in 1506. 'Yet', reported Dürer, 'he is the best painter of them all'.

Transferred from panel, 26½ × 34 (0·67 × 0·86). Purchased in 1857 from Achille Farina of the town of Faenza.

IOANNES BELLINVS

Giovanni BELLINI

(Active *ca.* 1459; died 1516)

He was the son of the painter Jacopo Bellini and brother of another painter, Gentile; his sister married Andrea Mantegna. There is no certain date of birth for Giovanni Bellini who lived and worked throughout his career at Venice. He seems to have been employed by the Venetian State first in 1479. He painted important work, later destroyed by fire, in the Doge's Palace at Venice and became the outstanding painter and teacher of his generation there. A superb example of his official portrait work is the *Doge Leonardo Loredan* (opposite) and the Gallery owns several fine examples of his treatment of a favourite theme, that of the Virgin and Child. Though there was probably some reciprocal influence, Bellini seems likely to have affected the style of both Giorgione (whom he outlived) and the young Titian (q.v.).

THE DOGE LEONARDO LOREDAN

One of Bellini's tasks, as it was later to be Titian's, required by the semi-official position he held at the Fondaco dei Tedeschi at Venice, was to paint the portrait of the Doge. The present picture probably originates in such a commission, likely to have been given around 1501 when Leonardo Loredan was elected Doge, and it seems full of discreet pride in the state as well as the sitter. He was aged sixty-five at his election. Loredan reigned for twenty years and represented the Venetian Republic at a period when Europe was leagued against her. Figurehead rather than actual ruler, the Doge always appeared in public in the stiff ceremonial clothes that Bellini here so beautifully depicts, and with a linen bonnet surmounted by the Ducal cap, the *corno*. Light plays gently but firmly about all the shapes, sculpting the few folds of the ivory-coloured, parchment-textured, patterned robe – and the folds and crinkles of the equally parchment-like skin of the old man encased in it. Everything seems certain and sure: from the great nut-like buttons that decorate the robe to the bright-eyed, steady gaze of the Doge who enshrines dignity, state-craft, and trust in the Venetian empire. If he is a figurehead, it is one worthy of the power that he represents. Yet all this is suggested rather than stated: it is contained within Bellini's marvellous image – which, at first glance, seems so simply devised and restricted in format. It is only a bust-length figure, set behind a parapet, and placed against a plain glowing background; one more Ducal portrait, and an official commission. Out of these elements Bellini has created one of the most famous of Venetian portraits. He has made Doge Loredan a symbol of the stability and splendour of Venice, and given him that immortality which the Renaissance rightly believed that only the artist can give.

Panel, 24¼ × 17¾ (0·615 × 0·45). Signed. Bought from William Beckford in 1844; in his collection probably by 1814, having previously belonged to Lord Cawdor (†1821) who acquired it from the Grimani Palace, Venice.

Albrecht ALTDORFER

(before 1480; died 1538)

He was probably born at Regensburg in Bavaria, where he certainly worked and where he died. He was active not only as painter and draughtsman but as an etcher, and also an architect. He became city architect at Regensburg and a town councillor there. Influenced by Dürer and presumably by Cranach (q.v.) Altdorfer became an independent, even revolutionary, artist and the leading painter of the 'Danube School'. There are one or two portraits by him, but his restricted painted *œuvre* chiefly comprises religious pictures, of great originality and sensitivity, and two pure landscape paintings – of which the present picture is one.

LANDSCAPE WITH A FOOTBRIDGE

Altdorfer is known to have travelled along the Danube in 1511 and the beautiful drawings that he then executed testify to his being fascinated by the tangled romantic landscape of the region. It becomes the setting, or background, in many of his pictures, but he responds to it with a lyrical expressionism which passes out of topographical accuracy. He is interested in the sky-scape as well as the landscape: catching subtle dawn effects with light-fringed clouds, and also the aerial blueness of sparklingly clear days when the trees seem taller and more freshly green, and the earth is uninhabited by man. It is a mood that Dürer had seized in his early watercolours, but which had then remained private – so many sheets from the artist's own sketchbook. What Altdorfer achieved was to make this the complete subject of a painting. In the present picture nothing interferes with the sense of nature growing; the moss-grown, deserted building at the left and the precarious bridge almost suggest man's retreat before the phenomenon of nature reclaiming its own. The trees foam wildly and the stream bubbles at the foot of the rocks half-screened by bushes. Only in the distant valley, amid the trees, gleams the thin spire of a church, with suggestions of a village nearby. It is the wildness that appeals to Altdorfer and which leads him to become a pioneer in landscape painting. In the history of art his achievement had little influence. During the 17th century, a great age of landscape painting, perhaps only his countryman Elsheimer was aware of his work. But Altdorfer is one of those artists – like Botticelli and Watteau – who are isolated and unexpected, and utterly personal; genius is always making nonsense of the history of art.

Vellum on panel, 16½ × 14 (0·420 × 0·355). Signed with monogram. Bought from Dr. Jacques Koerfer at Berne through Messrs. Nathan (Zürich) in 1961. At an earlier date in the possession of Messrs. Böhler at Munich; first recorded in a private collection at Aschaffenburg before 1910.

Andrea del SARTO

(1486-1530)

His correct name was ANDREA D'AGNOLO, but he was called *del Sarto* because of his father's trade as a tailor. He was born at Florence where he spent most of his life, apart from the years 1518-19 when he worked in France in the service of François I. He was apprenticed to Piero di Cosimo, according to Vasari, and was in partnership with Franciabigio. Apart from some portraits, he painted chiefly religious pictures.

The Gallery possesses a typical *Madonna and Child with SS. Elizabeth and John the Baptist* as well as the present portrait.

PORTRAIT OF A YOUNG MAN

It is understandable that this picture should once have been called a self-portrait, for its pose and atmosphere seem to suggest self-scrutiny. It is moody, challenging and yet somewhat withdrawn. Sarto is concerned not only with recording the features but with giving some sense of the sitter's personality. The position of the chair, the extreme turn of the head, away from the book he is holding, to confront the spectator – these increase the effect of immediacy. Whereas Bellini's *Doge Loredan* (Pl. 14) represents the quintessence of early Renaissance portrait ideals, an immobile image fixed in a timeless sphere by the clarity of the paint, Sarto's is the product of a later Renaissance concept. It emphasises time by the graceful yet marked action. The sitter does not merely look out of the picture but seeks for our eyes with his own. He emerges from a harmonious, silvery-dusky atmosphere which is almost as elusive as personality itself: emerging from it but remaining also wrapped in it, his clothes tinged with its dyes and even his features veiled by a misty tone. It is quite fitting that he has remained anonymous, so that the more freely the spectator can, as perhaps the painter once did, merge his own character with that of the sitter. And, like so many Florentine portraits of the period, the character it suggests in all its sober-suited, questioning, isolation is that of Hamlet.

Canvas, 28½ × 22½ (0·72 × 0·57). Signed with monogram. Bought in 1862 from the estate of Cavaliere Niccolo Puccini of Pistoia.

Lucas CRANACH

(1472-1553)

He was born in Upper Franconia at Kronach (whence his name). In 1502 he was taken into the service of the Elector Frederick of Saxony at Wittenberg and he continued to be active there during the reigns of the two succeeding Electors. He became a town councillor of Wittenberg and was twice made burgomaster. In 1552 he retired to Weimar, where he died the following year. Cranach painted portraits (including that of Titian, whom he met at Augsburg in 1550), allegorical and religious pictures and many mythological pictures in an enormous, studio-assisted, output during his long life.

The Gallery owns two small portraits by him, an allegory of Charity, and also a painting probably illustrating the legend of Wild Men, in addition to the recently-acquired picture here.

CUPID COMPLAINING TO VENUS

The impact of the Renaissance on Northern Europe is too easily forgotten amid the glamour of the Italian Renaissance. Cranach's picture is, however, an elegant reminder of the receptivity of some Northern courts to classical subject-matter - interpreted here with witty sophistication and also some moralising overtones. The concept was suggested by a poem of the third-century Greek poet, Theocritus, which tells of Cupid's complaint to Venus of being stung by bees when stealing a honeycomb. Lines in Latin at the top of the picture allude to this incident and add the reflexion that it is thus with human pleasure, always mixed with pain. None of this seems to weigh with the smiling Venus - naked but adorned with jewellery and a fashionable 16th century German hat - who wantonly breaks a bough of apples in a wonderfully dark wood that shelters a pair of deer. Venus and Cupid have wandered far from the Theocritean climate to this patently Northern world of pine forests, steep crags and romantic castles - *the* German dream that haunts its art right up to the 19th century. Cranach expresses also the German genius for, and its preference for, draughtsmanship. Everything is delineated with clarity, undramatically lit but traced with a wiry line that delights in slender bodies and sharp-pointed leaves and the jutting, impossible peak reflected in clear water. Colour is there only as addition: silhouetting shapes, enhancing the basically linear effect. This style - which requires the painter to be an accomplished draughtsman - is typical of European court art in the mid 16th century. Cranach takes his place along with Bronzino in Italy, Clouet in France and Hilliard in England.

Panel, 32 × 21½ (0·813 × 0·546). Bought in 1963 from Messrs. E. & A. Silbermann, New York. Before acquisition by the Silbermann Galleries it had been in a private collection since being sold in the E. Goldschmidt collection at Berlin in 1909.

Hans HOLBEIN the Younger

(1497/8-1543)

The younger Holbein was born at Augsburg, son of the painter Hans Holbein the Elder, under whom he was trained. He moved to Bâle and then to Lucerne; in 1519 he became a member of the painters' guild at Bâle. He is likely to have visited Italy about this time, and is known to have been in France in 1524. He set out for England in the late summer of 1526 and remained in London on this first visit some two years. In 1532 he was again in London where he now settled and by 1536 had entered the service of Henry VIII. Although chiefly famous for his portraits, Holbein executed designs for jewellery, pageants, etc., as well as fresco decorations.

The Gallery owns, in addition to *The Ambassadors*, the full-length *Christina of Denmark, Duchess of Milan*, which was painted in connection with Henry VIII's unsuccessful attempt to marry the sitter.

JEAN DE DINTEVILLE AND GEORGES DE SELVE ('THE AMBASSADORS')

The Arnolfini double-portrait is here echoed and expanded in composition, and *The Ambassadors* too is at once a document and a work of art. It records the friendship of two French diplomats who never actually served on embassy together: at the left Jean de Dinteville, ambassador to Henry VIII, and at the right Georges de Selve, Bishop of Lavaur, who in the spring of 1533 came to visit Dinteville in London. The picture is signed and dated that year. When Dinteville returned to France he took it with him to his château at Polisy – a name prominently included on one of the terrestrial globes which with other learned paraphernalia litter the what-not. Many explanations have been offered of the skull drawn in distortion across the foreground of the picture. A skull is a mortality symbol popular at the period, and sign of that vein of melancholy which especially in Northern countries accompanied Renaissance vigour. Both men here were precociously talented, but sick. Dinteville was soon prematurely forced by illness to retire from affairs and the Bishop died while still young. Holbein maps their faces carefully, yet with no more comment than he gives about the tessellated pattern of the floor. Light and shade are everywhere subordinated to line, despite the marvellous technical dexterity which renders all the surface of fur and silk and metal. Bourgeois at heart, Holbein is in some ways the Ingres of Tudor England and *Madame Moitessier* (Pl. 46) may be claimed as the spiritual sister of '*The Ambassadors*'.

Panel, 81½ × 82½ (2·07 × 2·095); signed and dated 1533. Bought from the Earl of Radnor in 1890. It had been sold into England at the end of the 18th century and purchased in 1808-9 by the Earl of Radnor. Previously recorded in France in various collections and originally at Polisy, the château of Jean de Dinteville.

Pieter BRUEGEL the Elder

(Active 1551; died 1569)

Neither the date nor place of Bruegel's birth is known, but he is recorded as a Master at Antwerp in 1551 and is known to have travelled to Rome and elsewhere 1552/3. Some ten years later he moved from Antwerp to Brussels. He must have been considerably influenced by Hieronymus Bosch (active 1480/1; died 1516), especially in his satirical and fantasy subjects; but his greatest works are his landscapes with their superb sensitivity to atmosphere. Recent scholarship has emphasised how sophisticated an artist Bruegel was, replacing the old legend of him as naive and 'peasant'. Bruegel's two sons Jan and Pieter were both painters, and he in fact founded a complete dynasty of artists.

THE ADORATION OF THE KINGS

The winter was long in Medieval and Renaissance times, especially in Northern Europe. 'My nose runs and the chimney smokes', says a medieval French poet, in effect, vividly evoking the draughty misery of that period. Dark forests, short days, cold rooms, all induce strange fantasies and Bruegel's *Adoration of the Kings* is easily recognized as product of a world very different from that Mediterranean atmosphere which produced sumptuous Venetian treatments of the theme. The scene here might be set in a fairground where grotesques and drolls have come to worship, still dressed in their elaborate tangled finery and bearing wonderful-looking presents of tinfoil and *papier-mâché*. Crowding about these people are peasants and soldiery as Bruegel saw them in the Netherlands of his day; and Christ is born into a tragi-comical world where already he is an object of suspicion. In other pictures Bruegel made this topicality quite explicit: his scene of the *Massacre of the Innocents*, for example, becomes the attack by Spanish soldiery on a Flemish village. It is unusual for him to paint a picture with no landscape in it, and the example here is not typical of what we prize in him most: wonderful sensibility to moods of landscape, under the changes of time and season. He responded to darkening winter afternoons, thick snow-storms – and autumn days too when the corn is heavy and golden – by painting these things with an intensity and feeling for natural effects never equalled.

Panel, 43¾ × 32¾ (1·11 × 0·835); signed and dated 1564. Bought from Guido Arnot in 1920, through the National Art-Collections Fund, and with a donation from that body. Previously in the collection of Georg Roth at Vienna; earlier mentioned as in a Viennese private collection, the property of a nobleman living in Prague.

MICHELANGELO

(1475-1564)

His name was MICHELANGELO BUONARROTI. He trained in Florence but increasingly worked in Rome, directly employed by successive Popes from Julius II onwards until the end of his life. His early works, and his chief interest, were in sculpture; for his last twenty or so years he was active largely as an architect. His principal paintings are the fresco decorations of the Sistine chapel (the ceiling and the *Last Judgement* over the altar) and the Cappella Paolina of the Vatican. His only certain easel painting is the *Doni Tondo* (Uffizi, Florence) which dates from about 1505.

Apart from the attributed picture below, the Gallery owns an unfinished *Entombment* which is catalogued as by Michelangelo, to whom it was already ascribed before the end of the seventeenth century.

THE MADONNA AND CHILD WITH S. JOHN AND ANGELS

A popular question about the authorship of pictures is: how do we *know* who painted them? In the present instance, we cannot be at all sure that Michelangelo was the painter. Several scholars have doubted the attribution and suggested alternative, though largely anonymous, artists. This is one of the many cases in which each eye must make its own decision, but the picture is worth such an effort. It is full of sculptural elements and is conceived as a bas relief – an effect enhanced by the polished treatment of the bronze-coloured flesh and the almost marble draperies. While in some places there are rather awkward motifs – like the Child placing a foot in the fold of the Madonna's robe – there are also passages of great beauty. The two angels at the right, twining together to make the effect of a single sinuous figure, have a concentration and harmony that is classical, and which suggests the work of a great artist. However, the bitter, enigmatic expression of the Madonna and the weight of her head contrast disconcertingly with the somewhat tortured and unsatisfactory realisation of her body which dissipates the monumental effect. Neither the Child nor S. John the Baptist seems to fit into the monumental idiom, so flatly are they conceived and with almost affected linear convolutions – most strikingly in the bristling pelt worn by the Baptist. If Michelangelo is the creator of the picture, it must have been an early work. It is unfinished and perhaps was left so because of the artist's dissatisfaction. At the same time, the most masterly passage of all is the barely begun portion of the two left-hand angels – silhouettes that might have stepped from a Greek vase. Perhaps this beauty is accidental: it is nevertheless a real one.

Panel, 41½ × 30¼ (1·05 × 0·76). Bought in 1870 from the executors of Lord Taunton. It had earlier been in the collection of H. Bonar who had brought it to England from Rome in about 1829. It seems to be the picture mentioned at Villa Borghese, Rome, at the end of the seventeenth century.

TITIAN

(Active before 1511; died 1576)

His proper name is TIZIANO VECELLIO. He was born at Cadore, in the mountains above Venice, but the exact date of birth is not known. He probably worked with Giorgione in Venice on the now obliterated frescoes on the Fondaco dei Tedeschi, and the two painters' early styles are very similar. Titian soon became not only the leading painter of Venice but a European figure – patronised outside Italy especially by the Emperor Charles V and his son Philip II of Spain.

Titian painted every type of picture – portraits, altarpieces, mythologies – in a career of enormous length. The Gallery possesses ten pictures by him, including the group portrait of the *Vendramin Family*, the early '*Noli Me Tangere*' and the small late *Madonna and Child*.

BACCHUS AND ARIADNE

Whether as the mysterious and beautiful stranger of Euripides' play or more obviously as the cheerful noisy wine god, Bacchus for long haunted men's imagination. To Titian, and later to Tintoretto, he is a figure of pure poetry: exuberant here as he leaps from his chariot upon the startled Ariadne, or tenderly rising from the sea to crown her with stars. It was for Alfonso d'Este, Duke of Ferrara, that Titian painted the *Bacchus and Ariadne*, last of three classical pictures for one of the Duke's 'alabaster rooms' in the castle at Ferrara. So eagerly awaited by the Duke, it took long to complete. At Venice his agent continually conveyed to Titian the cajolings, bribes, and threats which the desperate Duke despatched in the hope of having the picture finished. It was worth waiting for. Although a heavy yellow varnish now obscures the picture's silvery tones, nothing can obscure its superb effect. It is something quite new in Venetian art. To the opulent colour and sensuous feeling for the natural world that Bellini had already shown, Titian adds his own triumphant vigour. His picture is a riot of interwoven forms all rushing towards the left of the composition where Ariadne's pose and gesture check them. Freedom is epitomized in the streaming silver-crimson drapery of Bacchus: as it were, Titian's flag of conquest, painted with a new freedom too in the actual handling of oil paint. Titian had more than forty years' more activity when this picture was finished; he could equal but not eclipse its achievement.

Canvas, 69 × 75 (1·75 × 1·9); signed.   Bought from Thomas Hamlet in 1826. Sold into England at the very end of the 18th century from Villa Aldobrandini at Rome; it had been sent to Rome by the Papal Legate, Cardinal Pietro Aldobrandini, in 1598 when the state of Ferrara passed to the Papacy. Earlier in the castle at Ferrara for which it had been painted.

TITIAN

(Active before 1511; died 1576)

His proper name is TIZIANO VECELLIO. He was born at Cadore, in the mountains above Venice, but the exact date of birth is not known. He probably worked with Giorgione in Venice on the now obliterated frescoes on the Fondaco dei Tedeschi, and the two painters' early styles are very similar. Titian soon became not only the leading painter of Venice but a European figure – patronised outside Italy especially by the Emperor Charles V and his son Philip II of Spain.

Titian painted every type of picture – portraits, altarpieces, mythologies – in a career of enormous length. The Gallery possesses ten pictures by him, including the group portrait of the *Vendramin Family*, the early '*Noli Me Tangere*' and the small late *Madonna and Child*.

THE VENDRAMIN FAMILY

When Lord Arundel's son was in Italy in 1636, he heard of 'a picture of Titian at Venice to bee sould for five or 6 hundred duccatts'. Almost certainly this is the picture, which until then had remained in the Vendramin family. A year or two after it reached England and was owned by Van Dyck; and its effortless combination of dignity with intimacy is very much what Van Dyck tried to give his sitters. The incident which brings the male members of the Vendramin family to adore a reliquary of the True Cross is the privilege accorded by heaven to their ancestor, Andrea Vendramin; the reliquary was presented to him as head of a Venetian confraternity, later fell into a canal and remained suspended above the water until he was permitted to plunge in and rescue it. In Titian's picture, later generations of the family are gathered to beg the continued favour of heaven – and they had considerable commercial interests. Titian was at the height of his powers when it was painted, probably about 1543. The textures of hair and fur, silk and velvet, are each conveyed with broad and yet beautifully controlled brush strokes; the opulence is more sombre than Bellini's (as in Plate 13), but the medium of oil paint is used with staggeringly new freedom. Perhaps nothing reveals better Titian's confidence in his own mastery than the first thoughts – such as the head in the sky at the extreme left – which are still partly visible; he undertook the large canvas with many ideas yet to be resolved and created the superb solution while he painted.

Canvas, 81 × 118½ (2·06 × 3·01). Bought from the Duke of Northumberland, with the aid of a Special Grant and contributions from Samuel Courtauld, Sir Joseph Duveen and the National Art-Collections Fund, in 1929. It had been acquired by the tenth Earl of Northumberland in 1645-6 from the executors of van Dyck. Previously in Venice until at least 1636 and originally in the collection of the Vendramin family.

Jacopo TINTORETTO

(1518-1594)

His name was JACOPO ROBUSTI, but he took the nickname *Tintoretto* from his father's trade of dyer (*tintore*). He was born at Venice and is only once recorded as leaving it – in 1580 when he was at Mantua. The influence of Michelangelo (q.v.) and Titian (q.v.) was very strong on his work; from these disparate sources he evolved his own highly personal style. Although he painted portraits, and some mythological and historical pictures, he was particularly a painter of large scale religious pictures. The most famous assembly of his work is in the Scuola di S. Rocco at Venice for which he worked at varying periods of his life.

As well as the present picture, the Gallery possesses three other paintings by him, including a mythology (*The Origin of the Milky Way*) and a portrait.

S. GEORGE AND THE DRAGON

To this familiar subject, popular with painters and their patrons, Tintoretto brings his own concept, one very typical of him. Everything is dynamically agitated at the moment of collision between the charging saint and the dragon. In the foreground the princess seems poised for further flight away from this fretted coastline of swirling water and tossing trees. The whole cosmos is involved and the sky splits open in a white radiance, at the centre of which is a mysterious heavenly figure. It is by the power of God that S. George overcomes the dragon, and the vision thus reminds the spectator of God's constant wakeful presence amid the affairs of mankind. Tintoretto was always interested in such supernatural effects, dramas of divine intervention: interested both as artist and as man. He was eager to serve the Church, to express a faith, both religious and artistic, in the efficacy of miracles. No painter before him had made such sustained drama out of these miraculous moments where the dark solidity of earthly things is suddenly irradiated by spiritual shafts of light and the abrupt appearance of angels or saints. Tintoretto begins, as it were, with the firm scaffolding of earth: creating in this picture the wild coast, the stormy trees, the high buildings in the distance, to form an environment for S. George and the princess. But all this is in contrast to the visionary sky, painted with instinctive joy in the luminosity of light, where paint becomes almost insubstantial in its capturing of shimmering waves of brightness.

That miraculous infraction of nature's order – the symbol of Divine victory – is a vision seen not by the participants in the picture but by the spectator alone.

Canvas, 62 × 39½ (1·575 × 1·003). In the Rev. Holwell Carr bequest, 1831; it had belonged to him at least since 1821. Earlier in the collection of Richard Westall and in a London Sale in 1764 when said to come from the Cornaro family.

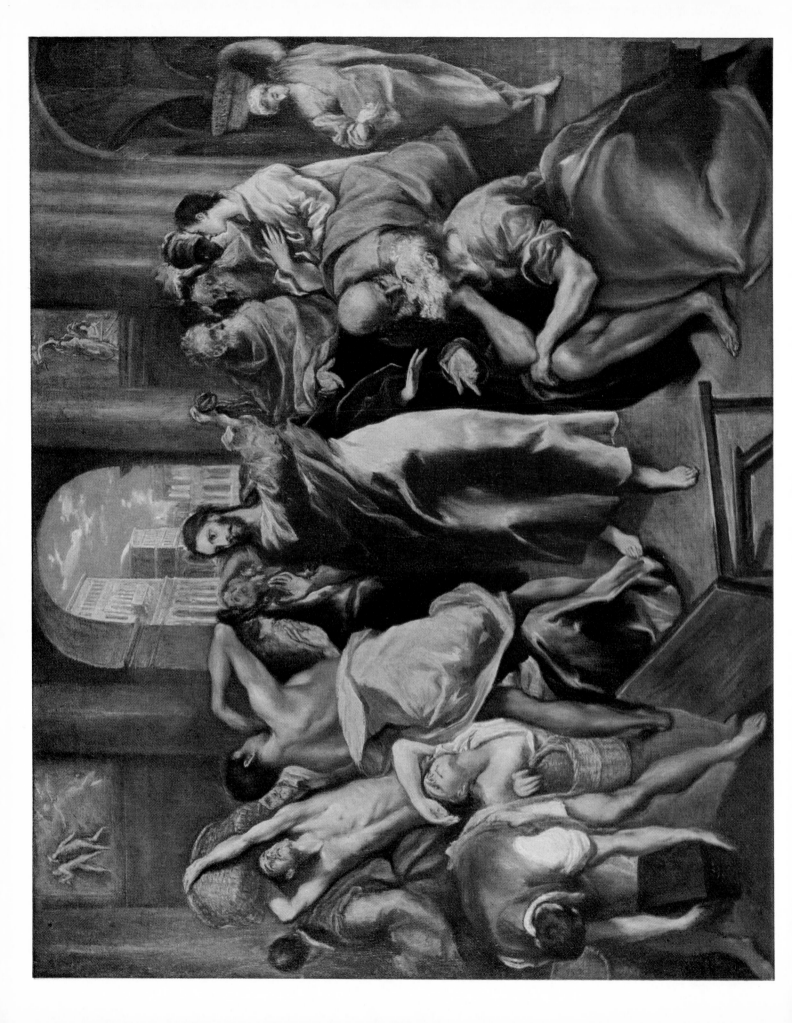

El GRECO

(1541-1614)

His proper name was DOMENIKOS THEOTOKOPOULOS. The usual form of his name nowadays means 'the Greek'. He was born in Crete which was then part of the Venetian Empire and he seems to have been a pupil of Titian's at Venice; there is also an influence apparent in his work from Tintoretto and Jacopo Bassano. He probably arrived in Rome late in 1570 but by 1577 he was in Toledo, where he settled for the rest of his life. Nothing is known of why he went to Spain, but his work failed to please Philip II. He executed pictures for churches and convents throughout Spain. He died in Toledo.

The Gallery possesses two other pictures by El Greco, including the *modello* for the large Escorial painting of the *Adoration of the Name of Jesus* which was probably among Greco's earliest Spanish works.

CHRIST DRIVING THE TRADERS FROM THE TEMPLE

El Greco had settled at Toledo by 1577, and his house there is now a museum. Coming from Crete, studying in Italy, and working in Spain, he betrays something of this complex interaction of influences in his art. Toledo today is full of his pictures – too full; and the mannerism of much he produced is repetitious and tiresome. The present picture, painted about 1600, is only one version of a composition he often repeated. Three great painters are part source for it: Raphael, Michelangelo and Titian. (El Greco apparently studied directly under Titian yet his work was disliked by Philip II of Spain, Titian's steady patron.) The painter has blended and concealed his sources, and the dynamic result is his alone. The eye is drawn directly to the intense flame-like figure of Christ which seems to quiver with nervous energy as he turns upon the traders. There is a general impression of violence which comes in fact from Christ alone but which runs through the confused gesticulating traders at the left, and is echoed by the more static but still gesticulating onlookers at the right. Christ himself seems lit by a lightning flash, and the whole picture has the distortion of a scene glimpsed at such a moment. It is more effective as a *coup d'oeil* than when closely examined. The scratchy brush strokes are typical of El Greco, and typical too are the simple colours, moon-blanched but roughly laid on.

Canvas, 41⅞ × 51⅛ (1·063 × 1·297). Presented to the Gallery by Sir J. C. Robinson in 1895. Previously sold at Christie's in 1877 when bought by Robinson and possibly one of the paintings of the same subject which are mentioned in the inventories of El Greco and his son Jorge Manuel.

CARAVAGGIO

(1573-1610)

MICHELANGELO MERISI was born at Caravaggio, a small town in Lombardy, from which he takes his name. After apprenticeship with an obscure Milanese painter, Peterzano, he went to Rome, probably about 1590, and quite soon found important patrons there. He received commissions for paintings in the Contarelli chapel of S. Luigi dei Francesi and the Cerasi chapel at S. Maria del Popolo, and painted other altarpieces and genre pictures. The increasing riotousness of his life created scandal at Rome and after a brawl in 1606 he fled to Naples and then to Malta – painting pictures at both places. In 1608/9 he was at work in Sicily; he returned to the Italian mainland and died of fever at Porto Ercole, aged not quite thirty-seven.

THE SUPPER AT EMMAUS

In his own period Caravaggio's pictures were thought shocking. Much could be said in favour of that point of view. Among the things originally criticized in the painting here were the rustic Apostles and the dish of fruit out of season. More alarming today is the academic and sentimental head of Christ, not realistic but anticipation of pious 19th-century oleographs. Nor was Caravaggio's 'realism' such as to make him disdain grand gestures; while his Apostles may be rustic in appearance, their behaviour is melodramatic. Christ might be dropping a bomb on the table, to judge from their reactions. Caravaggio is sometimes mentioned as a precursor of Rembrandt in treating incidents from the Bible in everyday terms. Rembrandt's *Supper at Emmaus* is a moving and simple scene in which Christ breaks bread with an almost weary benevolence: only gradually manifested as the Deity. Caravaggio's rhetoric appears inflated against that conception; and to explain the divergences in the two painters' attitudes would require a book. Caravaggio's dramatic moment immediately associates the spectator with the Apostles; Christ enjoins participation at the table, and we come within the sphere of his action as the audience at a theatre are caught up by events on the stage. Such emotional participation is reminiscent of the type of meditation proposed by Saint Ignatius Loyola in his 'Spiritual Exercises', written some thirty years before Caravaggio's birth. There is the same deliberate if unhealthy excitement of the imagination and the same emphasis upon realizing each physical detail of sacred history.

Canvas, 55 × 77½ (1·39 × 1·95). Presented to the Gallery by Lord Vernon in 1839. Previously for long in the Borghese collection, Rome, and acquired by Cardinal Scipione Borghese, an early collector of Caravaggio's work. The picture was painted for Ciriaco Mattei, along with other pictures by Caravaggio.

Sir Peter Paul RUBENS

(1577-1640)

Born at Siegen in Westphalia, but of Flemish parents. He was trained at Antwerp under several painters including Otto van Veen and then travelled to Italy where he became court painter to the Duke of Mantua: during this service he visited and worked at Rome and in Spain. In 1609 he returned to Antwerp where he settled. Increasingly involved in diplomatic activities, he travelled widely: to Paris, again to Madrid, and to London where he was knighted in 1630 by Charles I. Ceaselessly active both as artist and diplomat, Rubens had a European career of unparalleled scope and produced portraits, landscapes, mythological and religious pictures.

The Gallery possesses examples of his work in all three categories (see pls. 27 and 28 in addition to the picture here) but lacks anything on the large scale which Rubens handled so magnificently.

THE CHÂTEAU DE STEEN

In the last years of his life Rubens sought a retreat from Antwerp and from affairs in the country house of Steen at Elewyt, a building which still survives. Even there he did not fail to paint, and the rich wooded countryside was captured in pictures of which this is one of the most splendidly elaborate. Autumn is everywhere: as the trees turn and a sportsman with his dog stalks the partridges. The fecund season is symbolic of Rubens' own late fecundity. At the left is the moated, turreted château. No longer is landscape merely the setting for some religious or classical scene. It is a subject in its own right. Rubens' freshness and vigour, bold grasp of detail and superb assurance, are everywhere apparent. Beyond the writhing tangled undergrowth of the foreground the expanse of countryside, watered by streams and criss-crossed by clumps of trees, extends to that sky which is Rubens' most extraordinary achievement. Nobody before him had painted such an atmospheric effect, and nobody after him was to succeed – except Turner. These effects become even bolder in other late landscapes by Rubens, while the actual countryside becomes more intimate and less panoramic. In place of the daylight flooding the present picture, we are given evening landscapes where a solitary shepherd pipes to his flock and where the white-hot disk of setting sun hangs low in the sky. After a career as great decorator and portrait-painter, Rubens turned to his own Flemish countryside and once again achieved masterpieces.

Panel, 54 × 92½ (1·37 × 2·34). Presented by Sir George Beaumont as part of his Gift, 1823-8. It had been bought by Lady Beaumont as a present for her husband, having been imported into England in 1802 from Palazzo Balbi at Genoa.

Sir Peter Paul RUBENS

(1577-1640)

Born at Siegen in Westphalia, but of Flemish parents. He was trained at Antwerp under several painters including Otto van Veen and then travelled to Italy where he became court painter to the Duke of Mantua: during this service he visited and worked at Rome and in Spain. In 1609 he returned to Antwerp where he settled. Increasingly involved in diplomatic activities, he travelled widely: to Paris, again to Madrid, and to London where he was knighted in 1630 by Charles I. Ceaselessly active both as artist and diplomat, Rubens had a European career of unparalleled scope and produced portraits, landscapes, mythological and religious pictures.

The Gallery possesses examples of his work in all three categories (see Pls. 26 and 28 in addition to the picture here) but lacks anything on the large scale which Rubens handled so magnificently.

THE JUDGEMENT OF PARIS

Sometimes thought to have belonged to Cardinal Richelieu, this picture was certainly quite early in France and is exactly the sort of Rubens to inspire Watteau and Boucher. Its sumptuous delight in the female nude, brilliant colour and lively handling make the picture almost more rococo than baroque. Rubens more than once painted the subject which offered opportunities for his most opulent effects. In this version, the most mature, he seizes speedily on the pagan aspect of the story (but pagan in its literal Latin sense of country). His instinctive feeling for life embraces not only the nude goddesses but the fields and trees of Flemish landscape where he sets the classical scene. The picture is painted with immense vigour and spontaneity, forms thrown upon the panel with an assured draughtsmanship that fluently creates a bough, a drapery, an arm, until the whole picture is quivering with animation. Exultant pleasure in the senses is expressed throughout it, nowhere more superbly than in the Juno whose bare back is framed by the great sweep of fur robe. The three goddesses are like three studies from the same nude model, viewed frontally, in profile and from behind: delighting the spectator and dazzling Paris. Rubens had admired Titian's pictures in Italy, and had copied some of them. He is indeed the inheritor of Titian's vitality, the first and greatest Northerner to be endowed with Southern sensuousness, and the last Renaissance painter.

Panel, 57¼ × 76⅜ (1·45 × 1·94). Bought at the Penrice sale, London, in 1844. Previously in the collection of Lord Kinnaird who had been a past-buyer of the Orléans collection at the end of the 18th century. It is first certainly recorded in the Duc d'Orléans collection at the Palais-Royal in Paris in 1727.

Sir Peter Paul RUBENS

(1577-1640)

Born at Siegen in Westphalia, but of Flemish parents. He was trained at Antwerp under several painters including Otto van Veen and then travelled to Italy where he became court painter to the Duke of Mantua: during this service he visited and worked at Rome and in Spain. In 1609 he returned to Antwerp where he settled. Increasingly involved in diplomatic activities, he travelled widely: to Paris, again to Madrid, and to London where he was knighted in 1630 by Charles I. Ceaselessly active both as artist and diplomat, Rubens had a European career of unparalleled scope and produced portraits, landscapes, mythological and religious pictures.

The Gallery possesses examples of his work in all three categories (see pls. 26 and 27 in addition to the picture here) but lacks anything on the large scale which Rubens handled so magnificently.

'LE CHAPEAU DE PAILLE'

The hat is not made of straw, as visitors to the Gallery never fail to point out. But the title has a respectable ancestry and the picture has for long been famous. When the picture was eventually bought for England in the early nineteenth century, the rage of Antwerp at its loss is said to have been great. It is recorded in Rubens' effects after his death; later Louis XV apparently tried to acquire it; George IV is said to have admired it. The sitter so vividly created by Rubens' brush is not known, and her name hardly matters. She is a tribute first to the unfailing power of Rubens' creativity. As superbly as ever he has responded to blonde flesh, to female vitality, investing the sitter with extraordinary and eternal vividness. The face is slightly shaded by the broad-brimmed, feather-trimmed hat. The pearly tone of the flesh is seen at its whitest on the neck and breasts, and is superbly set off by the black, grayish green and red draperies. Across the face the shadow is faint and milky, barely perceptible; the quick candid gaze of the eyes takes attention from any-thing else. The oil paint seems laid on almost impatiently – the sky hastily brushed in, the hair flying, and the curled feathers on the hat writhing like sea creatures. Every part of the picture quivers with intensity. It is still charged with the electric force of Rubens' genius, as if only a moment ago he completed the picture and flung down his brush.

Panel, 30½ × 21 (0·77 × 0·53). Bought with the collection of Sir Robert Peel, 1871. He had purchased the picture from a London dealer in 1823, it having been sold the previous year in Antwerp from the estate of Baron Stiers d'Aertselaer. Earlier in the possession of the Lundens family who had inherited the picture at Rubens' death in 1640.

Nicolas POUSSIN

(1594?–1665)

Poussin was born near Les Andelys in Normandy, studied for a period in Paris and then settled in Rome in 1624. He visited Paris in 1641/2 but was not happy there and returned to Rome where he died. Italian art exercised a significant influence on him: not only that represented by contemporary artists, of whom Domenichino was the chief, but the work also of Titian (q.v.). And in Rome Poussin was in direct contact with the monuments of classical antiquity. From all these elements he created a unique style.

The Gallery possesses several other paintings by Poussin, which help to trace his evolution from the Venetian-poetic *Cephalus and Aurora* (painted about 1630) to the highly organised spatial world of the *Landscape with a Snake* (1648), and including an example of his late style in *The Annunciation* (dated 1657).

BACCHANALIAN REVEL BEFORE A TERM OF PAN

The greatest French painter of the 17th century lived most of his life in Rome. In that century hardly a great painter but came to the city, either briefly like Velázquez and Rubens or, like Poussin, to live and stay. And it was at Rome that Caravaggio had, before the century began, achieved an extraordinary revolution in realism (Pl. 25). Poussin was to achieve something very different. Devout Christian and passionate classical scholar, he was to depict with serious attention and dignified imagination the two worlds of religious and pagan antiquity: these met in Poussin's pictures as they met – and meet – in Rome. At first glance his *Bacchanal* may seem a cold pastoral against the stupendous vigour of Titian, whose work Poussin much admired and copied. It is an exercise in formal logic set amid Titianesque landscape: the figures interwoven like those of a classical frieze, the trio of dancers at the left linked into a complicated rhythmic pattern which Poussin was to re-create even more superbly. In a later picture (in the Wallace Collection), the *Dance to the Music of Time*, a quartet of figures tread out their steps with measured motion, observing a solemn and eternal rite. In the *Bacchanal* there is all the spontaneity of a bibulous frolic, and beneath the restraint immense verve; the dancing trio, however decorous, have great gaiety. It is this which is essentially Poussin's gift: to have achieved, as French classical drama achieves, that balanced harmony whereby under a formal exterior is the beat of life itself.

Canvas, 39¼ × 56¼ (1·00 × 1·425). Bought from the jeweller Thomas Hamlet, the owner also of Titian's *Bacchus and Ariadne*, in 1826. Previously in several English sales, having been sold in London in 1795; it is recorded earlier in the 18th century in French sales. Traditionally said to have come from a palace at Rome, and also to have been ordered from Poussin by Cardinal Richelieu.

Diego VELAZQUEZ

(1599-1660)

His name in full was DIEGO RODRÍGUEZ DE SILVA VELAZQUEZ. He was born in Seville and studied under Francisco Pacheco, whose daughter he married. His first visit to Madrid was briefly in 1622, but he was there again the following year. The success of his first portrait of the king, commissioned in 1623, resulted in his becoming royal painter and thus spending the rest of his life at the Madrid court where he held ceremonial posts in addition to his duties as painter. In 1629 he left Spain for his first visit to Italy and twenty years later made another journey there, painting the portrait of *Pope Innocent X* at Rome in 1650. His most famous picture, *Las Meninas* (Prado, Madrid), was apparently completed in 1656. He was made a knight of Santiago in 1659, the year before his death.

Among its outstanding group of pictures by Velazquez, the Gallery owns the well-known *Rokeby Venus* – one of Velazquez's rare surviving mythological pictures – as well as a portrait of Philip IV in middle age.

PHILIP IV IN BROWN AND SILVER

Philip IV was probably about twenty-six when he posed for this portrait on Velazquez's return to Madrid from Italy. Velazquez was back in Spain by 1631 and during his absence the King is recorded not to have allowed any other painter to portray him. This portrait shows him dressed with unusual splendour, in a costume of almost shimmering brilliance, and the picture is full of formal overtones: from the public-image sense of the figure, with cloak and sword, and hat lying on the table behind, to the paper held in the gloved right hand. This is inscribed with the opening words of a petition from Velazquez to the King and at the same time it provides a signature – something very rare indeed in Velazquez's work. The official nature of the portrait is emphasised by the immobile pose; there is an almost timeless sense of the King standing there, impassive, already a little weary, his face blank of emotion. Majesty and vacuity are combined – perhaps accidentally, but it is impossible not to feel in the large Gallery of royal portraits created by Velazquez a somnolent boredom and emptiness in the personages. The splendid clothes here enhance the effect of a vacuum covered and adorned. Velazquez makes no comment, but he records unfalteringly what he sees. He is true to that standard. His marvellous technique matches his eye and gains increasing freedom to paint what is seen rather than what is known to be there. The silver embroidery in this picture is suggested by brilliant streaks of paint which give vitality to the costume and make a suitable foil to the more carefully recorded, flaccid, features.

Canvas, *c.* 78½ × *c.* 43¼ (1·95 × 1·30); signed. Bought for the Gallery at the Duke of Hamilton sale, London, 1882. Previously in the collection of William Beckford, whose daughter had married the 10th Duke of Hamilton, and in that of General Dessolle (†1828) to whom it was given by Joseph Bonaparte in about 1810, having previously hung in a Spanish royal palace.

REMBRANDT

(1606-1669)

His full name was REMBRANDT HARMENSZ. VAN RIJN. He was the son of a miller and was born at Leyden where he was inscribed as a student at the University in 1620. He studied painting at Leyden and then moved to Amsterdam, studying for some time under Pieter Lastman. Amsterdam remained his home for the rest of his life and, at least for a period, he was a popular and very busy portrait-painter there. From about 1640 onwards his commissions seem to have dwindled but he remained very active – as draughtsman and etcher, as well as painter -- and it is in the last years of his life that the greatest of his works originate.

The Gallery possesses twenty pictures by Rembrandt. They show not only the development of his style over a period of some forty years but the range of his art: from the baroque drama of *Belshazzar's Feast* to the dignified simplicity of the aged *Margaretha Trip*, including also two self-portraits.

SASKIA VAN ULENBORCH IN ARCADIAN COSTUME

Rembrandt married Saskia van Ulenborch in 1634. The orphaned cousin of Rembrandt's landlord at Amsterdam, Saskia brought the painter not only happiness but considerable wealth. The years of their marriage coincided with an increase in Rembrandt's own fame and position as an artist. In many portraits, painted and drawn and etched, Saskia appears under different guises or simply as herself. She became Rembrandt's inspiration and obsession, sometimes to be found in pictures that are not portraits. Here she appears perhaps as Flora, at least as incarnation, it seems, of fertility. In rather similar clothes but with her head heavily garlanded with flowers, she stands in a picture at Leningrad. But here she is more bountiful and beneficent; a blonde light bathes her face and neck and throws the shadow of her sheaf of flowers over the white skirt. It does not really matter what Saskia is dressed up to represent; her costume is a timeless fancy dress which Rembrandt has devised. But as she emerges so firmly out of the dark foliage and shadows of the background, it is tempting to see her as Proserpina returning with the spring. This triumphant appearance was tragically brief. Rembrandt's portraits begin to trace the decline of Saskia's health; she no longer poses for pictures, but many drawings show her bed-ridden, ailing or recovering from child-birth. In 1641 their son Titus was born, the only child of Rembrandt's who lived; the next year Saskia died, aged barely thirty. No premonition touches this splendid radiant figure.

Canvas, 48⅝ × 38⅜ (1·235 × 0·975).   Bought from the 8th Duke of Buccleuch in 1938, with a contribution from the National Art-Collections Fund. Inherited by the 3rd Duchess of Buccleuch in 1790 from her father, the Duke of Montagu, for whom it had probably been bought at the Duc de Tallard Sale at Paris in 1756.

CLAUDE

(1600–1682)

His full name was CLAUDE GELLEE, often called Le Lorrain. He was born at Champagne in the Vosges but was in Rome already by about 1613 and virtually remained there for the rest of his long life. His pictures are always landscapes, with figures sometimes perhaps added by other hands but generally by Claude himself. Within the apparent restriction of his subject-matter there is great variety, evolution, and sensitivity to changing atmosphere. He had many important patrons, both in France and Italy, during his career. In the 18th and 19th centuries he was particularly esteemed in England, was much collected, and exercised considerable influence on English painters.

The Gallery possesses eleven pictures by him, nearly all early purchases or gifts, ranging in date from 1632 to 1671.

LANDSCAPE: CEPHALUS AND PROCRIS REUNITED BY DIANA

Claude was born in the year Rubens arrived in Italy. While still a boy he too arrived in Italy where he was to remain, with one interruption, for the rest of his long life. This signed and dated picture (dated at Rome, 1645) is a landscape of the Roman Campagna in which the mythological trio at the right have little relevance. Nor is it a piece of literal topography. As Goethe said, Claude knew the real world but used it to express the world of his own spirit. It is the Campagna recollected in tranquillity: a serene countryside in subdued light, with cattle leisurely splashing through the ford while their herdsman lounges negligently along a fallen tree-trunk. The eye is slowly led by contrasts of light and shade to the golden horizon where long swathes of mist lie about the hills. In this timeless world the two lovers united by the goddess are a reminder of classical antiquity, as would be a Roman tombstone or a ruined temple. The Campagna is full of Roman memories and Claude is as aware as Gibbon later was, of the continuity (and the poignancy) of that civilization half-buried in the grass where the shepherds graze their flocks. Claude is a poetic painter, but one who worked hard on the spot, making detailed drawings and apparently painting from nature – a revolution at the period. He lived in seclusion avoiding the official and social life of Rome; like his life, his art is circumscribed, but it gains intensity from this very restriction.

Canvas, 40 × 52 (1·02 × 1·32). Bought with the rest of the J. J. Angerstein Collection at the founding of the Gallery, 1824. It had been imported into England from France in 1795; previously in several important French collections and apparently first recorded in that of La Live de Jully (probably by 1757).

Bartolomé Esteban MURILLO

(1617-1682)

He was born in Seville, like Velazquez (q.v.), but unlike Velazquez he remained there for most of his life and died there. He certainly visited Madrid where the pictures of Rubens and van Dyck had a significant influence on his style, which moved from naturalism to an almost rococo decorative manner, with soft forms and sweetened colour. He painted series of pictures for religious foundations as well as genre pictures and a few rare portraits. His work enjoyed enormous popularity, and his reputation has suffered from an inevitable reaction which has tended to make him under-valued. He was much assisted by pupils and was copied and imitated; many pictures passing as his must be by other hands.

The Gallery possesses several pictures by him, including the dignified *Self Portrait* which is inscribed as painted at the wish of his children.

THE TWO TRINITIES

The appeal of this picture is obvious. A note need hardly explain anything in it except its slightly unusual subject, and remark that a long period of inglorious activity was about to occur in Spanish painting at the time it was painted. The subject is the two Trinities on heaven and earth linked by Christ. It seems to have developed out of pictures of Christ's return with His parents from the Temple but has here become the subject of a large devotional altarpiece. Cleaning of the picture has revealed charming colour – especially in the coral and greys of God the Father – but still does not quite explain the enormous vogue once enjoyed by Murillo. His reputation is now emerging again from reaction, partly owing to the discovery that many poor pictures in his style are not by him. The present picture is by him, however, and is even a splendid example of its type. When it was painted El Greco was of course long dead; Velazquez had died, and Zurbaran also. Murillo painted it late in his career, and after his death nothing of much interest happened until the emergence of Goya on the Spanish artistic scene late in the eighteenth century. Of all these, Murillo's talent is perhaps the least original and vigorous. His work is the product of a person awkwardly straddled between two periods: weaker and softer than the best painting of the seventeenth century (at times his style is like that of Rubens diluted with holy water) and in colour harmonies and airy compositions anticipating the eighteenth century. To some extent, it is by the decorative standards of the following century that Murillo must be judged.

Canvas 115¼ × c. 81½ (2·93 × c. 2·07). Bought by the Gallery in 1837 after having been exhibited in London that year at the George Yeates' Gallery. It had been brought to England around January 1810 and was previously in the Pedroso collection at Seville and at Cadiz (mentioned in the latter place in 1708).

Johannes VERMEER

(1632-1675)

Vermeer was the son of a silk-weaver who may at one time have been a dealer in works of art. He was born in Delft, married there in 1653 and died there – leaving a widow and eleven children. Little is known about him and there is even a sort of impersonality about his art. Not a large group of pictures exists by him; but though this is often said to indicate that he was a slow worker, as perhaps he was, it is also a reminder of his comparatively brief life and premature death. There is some Italian influence in his earliest pictures; he probably never visited Italy. He was greatly influenced by another short-lived, brilliantly original painter, Carel Fabritius, who was killed at Delft in 1654.

The Gallery owns one other picture by Vermeer apart from the present one, of virtually the same subject but with a woman shown seated at a virginal.

A YOUNG WOMAN STANDING AT A VIRGINAL

'Do you know', Van Gogh wrote to a friend, 'about a painter named Jan van der Meer?' And he goes on to describe Vermeer's palette as including blue, lemon yellow, pearl grey, black and white. This picture is only one piece of evidence of what Vermeer could achieve by use of such colours. The perfect stillness it breathes is matched by its perfection of cool tone. Light is almost congealed to hold within it this moment when the girl's fingers just touch the keys of the virginal. The picture is generally accepted as late work in Vermeer's short career, and is sometimes supposed to be among the pictures mentioned as owned by his widow. The mastery he had achieved is obvious enough. There is really no subject, and attempts to deduce significance from the prominent picture of Cupid in the background are not convincing. Rather similar pictures of Cupid are introduced by Vermeer into other paintings, perhaps with no more reason than here; and even if Cupid is meant to recall the deceitful aspect of love (as he holds up a playing card), the girl pointedly turns away from his message. There is no drama, except the eternal drama of light: Vermeer's interest in light is typical of all Dutch art and there are times when one thinks that all Dutch art is equivalent to Rembrandt. Rembrandt's own obsession with light effects had tremendous influence far beyond his own pupils. And Vermeer was only a boy of ten when the so-called *Night Watch* was painted.

Canvas, $20\frac{3}{8} \times 17\frac{13}{16}$ (0·517 × 0·452); signed. Bought in 1892, previously having been in the collection of the critic Thoré (who had done much to rediscover Vermeer) at least since 1866. Earlier in various sales in London and elsewhere. The first certain reference to it is presumed to be in a sale at Amsterdam in 1797.

Jacob van RUISDAEL

(1628 or 1629?; died 1682)

His name in full was JACOB ISAACKSZ. VAN RUISDAEL. He was born at Haarlem at a date not certainly established, though in a document of June 1661 he is said to be thirty-two. (Unfortunately, other painters' ages given in the same document are incorrect.) His father was an art-dealer, frame-maker and also a painter of landscapes – though none of his pictures can now be established with certainty. By June 1657 Ruisdael had settled at Amsterdam, but must have travelled a good deal in Holland, as identified views by him reveal. A somewhat surprising fact is that he apparently took a degree as a Doctor of Medicine at Caen in France, in October 1676, became inscribed on the list of Amsterdam doctors and is recorded as having performed surgical operations there. After the decade of 1660 there are no certain dated paintings. Ruisdael probably died in Amsterdam but he was buried at Haarlem.

The Gallery owns fourteen certain landscapes by him, as well as some other pictures in his style.

A WATERFALL IN A ROCKY LANDSCAPE

Although Ruisdael is usually and rightly associated with Dutch landscape, there is a group of pictures by him which shows his interest in a very different and much more dramatic landscape – one which he never presumably saw for himself. A slightly older painter, Allart van Everdingen, who worked at Haarlem and Amsterdam, seems to have visited some part of Scandinavia and it was he who introduced a new type of landscape picture into Holland: compositions like this one of rocky mountain scenery and tremendous waterfalls. The sheer difference of such wild scenes from the domestic tranquillity of their own countryside perhaps appealed to Dutch patrons – and also to Ruisdael. He obviously felt a great response to moody weather: dull days of heavy cloud, with oppressive breaks of thundery brightness, and grey days where the cold sea rolls in on bleak shores. To such subjects welcome drama is added by the romantic splendour of the Scandinavian countryside, especially for a painter who was free to imagine it. The tall pine trees, mountains, the great rocks over which torrents pour, are all exotic elements for him and he can assemble them into memorably oppressive scenes, where nature bleakly, and yet excitingly, dominates man. The very few tiny figures that are present here serve only to suggest the vastness and grandeur of nature. This is communicated most powerfully by the steel-grey water that rushes out of the picture, falling in sheets of foam in the foreground, boiling where the various currents mingle, and then sweeping rapidly on. Ruisdael's imaginative art creates a Scandinavia more vivid than any reality could be.

Canvas, 38¾ × 33½ (0·985 × 0·85). Bought in 1859 at the Graf Andreas von Stolberg Sale, Hanover. It had been passed to him in 1814 with the rest of the collection of Graf Friedrich Moritz von Brabeck who owned it by 1792.

Meyndert HOBBEMA

(1638-1709)

He was born in Amsterdam and seems to have adopted the name Hobbema. He was apprenticed to the great landscape painter Jacob van Ruisdael (q.v.) and he often followed Ruisdael's style very closely. He lived always in Amsterdam, though visits elsewhere seem likely, and died there. He painted only landscapes and exercised a considerable influence on English art in the 18th and 19th centuries.

Apart from *The Avenue*, his most famous picture, the Gallery possesses eight pictures by him which well display the range of his art and testify to English collectors' fondness for his work.

THE AVENUE, MIDDELHARNIS

It is often said that everyone has at least one good novel inside him, and perhaps there is a masterpiece inside every painter. Hobbema was fortunate enough to achieve his in this famous picture. Its fame is fully deserved, for its simple solution to the problem of composition is brilliantly effective; and the eye cannot resist being drawn up the avenue of tall straggling trees which leads to the village of Middelharnis. The pleasure of entering a picture in this way is a very real one. Not only has Hobbema discovered how to seize the attention immediately, but he has found a method of enlivening the flat Dutch countryside without romanticising its prosaic qualities. The trees not only mark the perspective of the road but emphasise the airy windy expanse of unsettled sky; the whole picture is touched by a transient effect of light and shadow – the day is one with a hint of rain on the wind. Such paintings make one understand Constable's debt to Dutch art. As for Hobbema, he had painted many other competent country scenes, but never before a masterpiece. From what we hear, he seems to have given up painting altogether well before the end of his life – probably because there was, for him as well as for other Dutch painters, little patronage. Nor do his other pictures even hint that he would be capable of achieving the masterpiece here. Perhaps we owe it to some lucky accident, to the effectiveness of the scene in itself. But an artist like Rubens takes his opportunities everywhere and does not need a happy accident.

Canvas, 40¾ × 55½ (1·035 × 1·41). Purchased with the collection of Sir Robert Peel in 1871. It had belonged to Peel by 1834 and had come from Holland some ten years previously, being exhibited for sale at Edinburgh. From 1782 to 1822 it was in the Town Hall at Middelharnis and is earlier recorded in the collection of Theodorus Kruislander who lived near Middelharnis.

CANALETTO

(1697-1768)

His full name was GIOVANNI ANTONIO CANAL. He was born at Venice, the son of a scene painter and designer with whom he collaborated as a young man. About 1720 he probably began his career as a viewpainter and soon became famous. Patronised especially by the English, he visited England in 1746 and, with brief returns to Venice, remained in England for some nine years. He returned to Venice and remained active until his death there.

By Canaletto, or from his studio, the Gallery owns fifteen view pictures, including the early *Stone Mason's Yard*, two English views, and a pair of small scenes of Piazza S. Marco which probably date from post 1755.

VENICE: THE BUCENTAUR AT THE PIAZZETTA

In Canaletto's Venice the Doge was still the titular ruler of the state just as he had been when painted by Bellini (pl. 14). His public life was a series of ceremonies which proclaimed the glory of Venice long after the reality of power had passed away and the city had become a tourist attraction. Every Ascension Day the Doge set out in his golden barge from the Piazzetta to be rowed across to the Lido where he performed the ceremony of wedding the sea, dropping into the waves a ring, and thus symbolising Venetian maritime supremacy. In the wonderful detail of Canaletto's crowded scene there can just be made out – at least in the original picture – the Doge's gold umbrella going forward through the massed spectators in the procession to board the bucentaur. But Canaletto steps back from the scene, to take in not so much the ceremony as the permanent parade of Venice itself: with its domes and bell towers, and its pink Doge's Palace, rising sheerly from the water into a crystalline sunlit atmosphere. Canaletto is often accused of being a prosaic painter, a mere recorder of cities before photography was invented. Yet this view of Venice is a vision rather than straightforward reality: with distance and atmosphere enhanced, with tremendous response to the fantasy of Venice which happens to be fact. Nor is Canaletto a painter only of buildings and water; in the foreground at the left there is the crisp miniature genre scene of the skiff with two seated ladies and a boatman holding over their heads a stretched yellow parasol that has a typically eighteenth century blend of wit and imagination.

Canvas, 48 × 72 (1·219 × 1·828). Bequeathed in 1929 by Lord Revelstoke who had bought it in 1923 from A. J. Sulley; he bought it at the Duke of Leeds sale, London, 1920. It is mentioned in the collection of the Duke of Leeds at Hornby Castle in 1867.

Jean-Baptiste-Siméon CHARDIN

(1699-1779)

He was born at Paris, where he worked all his life, and died there. He trained under several painters but evolved a style completely his own in treating genre and still life; he also painted a very few portraits. He became a member of the Académie Royale in 1728 and was a frequent exhibitor at the Salon; he held several official *Académie* posts and for some years was responsible for the hanging of the exhibitors' pictures at the Salon. In later life, owing to failing eyesight, he turned to pastel in preference to oil paint as a medium.

The Gallery possesses three pictures by Chardin, including *The House of Cards* which seems to have been conceived in composition as some sort of pendant to the present picture.

THE YOUNG SCHOOLMISTRESS

Everybody in 18th-century Paris appreciated Chardin's pictures. They are, indeed, some of the most easily enjoyed of great pictures. At the time there was a passing doubt about the suitability of showing maids and kitchen-boys and other low people engaged on humble tasks; but even this doubt disappeared when Chardin raised the social class of his characters. Here not only is there nothing vulgar or workaday, but the picture is a touching lesson in morality: the very subject is an education. One doesn't paint with colours, Chardin remarked snubbingly to an inquisitive questioner, '*mais avec le sentiment*'. Watteau could have said the same, but his resultant creation is almost too pointedly different. Chardin's power lay in lovingly sober delineation of what he saw. There is none of that dramatic effect which some feeling for some sort of 'realism' had prompted in Caravaggio. Chardin belongs rather by temperament with the Dutch painters of the 17th century, and like them he respects facts. Nobody else has managed to make so much out of a still life; pots and pans painted by Chardin are invested with more dignity and a great deal more interest than most human beings possess. The scene here is made more than charming by the integrity of each object; and the eye is delighted by the firm shapes of the caps, the open book, the desk, and the hard steel pointer the girl holds. Despite its intimate character and its attractive colour, the picture is austerely plotted and economically contrived with something of Poussin's intellectuality.

Canvas, 24¼ × 26¼ (0·616 × 0·665). Bequeathed to the Gallery as part of the John Webb Bequest, 1925, by his daughter Mrs. Edith Cragg. In the James Stuart Sale, London, 1850. Perhaps the version of the composition exhibited at the Salon in 1740.

Sir Joshua REYNOLDS

(1723-1792)

He was born at Plympton, near Plymouth, but came to London in 1740 when apprenticed to the painter Thomas Hudson. Between 1749-52 he was touring abroad, spending most of his time in Rome. He settled in London in 1753 and soon became the leading portrait painter of the day; he kept a busy studio and was much assisted by pupils and drapery painters. On the foundation of the Royal Academy in 1768, he became its first President. On the death of Allan Ramsay in 1784, he succeeded him as the King's Principal Painter, though in fact George III's private preference was Gainsborough (q.v.) as an artist. Reynolds' annual discourses to the Academy students form an important body of 18th century aesthetic theory and at the same time reveal his ability to respond to painters whose practice differed from his own.

The National Collection, held between the Tate and National Galleries, contains a representative selection of his work.

CAPTAIN ROBERT ORME

Writing to a friend in August 1755, Horace Walpole mentioned Captain Orme as someone who 'has made some noise here by an affair of gallantry'. This seems a reference to his interest in Audrey, daughter of Lord Townshend, whom he married apparently against her family's wishes. But in 1755 Captain Orme was also attracting some attention through being present at the death of General Braddock, killed by the French near Fort Duquesne (Pittsburgh); Orme was his aide-de-camp and was wounded in the same ambush – to which perhaps Reynolds makes some reference in the background of this picture (dated the following year). It has an air of panache and easy dignity: the swinging shape of the restless horse contrasted with the calm Orme, gazing out at the spectator. Reynolds responds to the gallant and martial air of his sitter, brushing in the face with a sort of nearly tender eagerness rather unexpected in a formal commission. Presumably Orme himself commissioned the picture, but for some reason it remained on Reynolds' hands and was shown by him at the Society of Artists exhibition in 1761. At the time it was painted Reynolds – like the sitter – was only in his early thirties. He was not yet so anxious as he became to emphasise the dignity and rank of his sitters. It is enough for him that Orme is young and brave. Perhaps Reynolds succeeds with him the better because he is a man; in general, his male portraits are superior to his female ones. Here there is a direct confrontation of painter and sitter, and this has left its faintly challenging air on the resulting portrait.

Canvas, 94½ × 58 (2·40 × 1·47). Signed and dated 1756. Bought at the Earl of Orkney Sale, London, 1862. Apparently descended in the family from the 5th Earl of Inchiquin who bought it from Reynolds in 1770.

Thomas GAINSBOROUGH

(1727-1788)

He was born at Sudbury in Suffolk where his house is now a small museum. Very early he came to London and received some training from the French engraver Gravelot, through whom he may have learnt of Watteau's work. About 1746 he returned to Sudbury and then moved to Ipswich, practising chiefly as a portrait painter and, at that period, usually on a small scale. In 1759 he moved with his family to the fashionable city of Bath, whence he sent pictures for exhibition at the newly established Royal Academy, of which he was a foundation member in 1768. In 1774 he moved to London and set up in Pall Mall; during the rest of his life he shared patronage with Reynolds, being the preferred portraitist of George III. He painted landscapes as well as portraits and, increasingly towards the end of his career, subject pictures.

A good range of his work is in the National Collection, held between the National and Tate Galleries.

THE MORNING WALK

England's claim to a great school of painting is not strong. It is the more unfortunate that it was in the 18th century that the native school at last produced some worthwhile work, for it is this century which is still misunderstood. Gainsborough has every claim to be considered England's greatest painter, but his very charm and elegance are un-English; and his graceful air of pleasing does not always find sympathetic spectators in a puritan nation. This superb picture, for example, often has to be apologised for and defended — just as Mozart once had to be defended against those who thought his music pretty but artificial. Of course the sitters here, a certain newly-married Mr. and Mrs. Hallett, are treated with artifice: everything has a silken texture, not only ribbons but even the leaves on the trees and the fine fur of the dog. The young couple advance like dancers in a set-piece of gauzy foliage and leafy drapery. The whole picture is 'pencilled' rather than heavily painted; we know that Gainsborough liked to use long-handled brushes and preserve a sketch-like quality even on large pictures such as this. Even Reynolds, who disapproved of the lack of finish, had to admit that from a distance Gainsborough's pictures appeared to be finished. In fact, this enchanting light touch unites Gainsborough to his great European contemporaries and helps to lift him outside the provincial confines of English art. Just as Watteau came to be denigrated in France, and Tiepolo despised in Italy, so Gainsborough takes his portion of neglect while he joins the other two as the greatest imaginative artists of their century.

Canvas, 93 × 70½ (2·36 × 1·79). Bought from Lord Rothschild, with a contribution from the National Art-Collections Fund, in 1954. In the Rothschild collection since 1884. Previously in the collection of the grandson of the sitters, W. E. Hilliard. Mentioned as offered for sale in London in 1834.

Francisco de GOYA

(1746-1828)

His full name was FRANCISCO JOSE DE GOYA Y LUCIENTES. Goya was born at Fuendetodos, near Saragossa, and studied first under a minor painter at Saragossa. In 1766 he was in Madrid where he became a pupil of Francisco Bayeu, whose sister he married in 1773. Two years later he had settled in Madrid and from 1776 worked on a series of cartoons for the Royal Tapestry establishment. In 1786 he was made painter to the king and he executed portraits of many members of the royal family, including the group portrait of *Charles IV and his family* (Prado, Madrid). The upheavals at the end of the 18th century and the arrival of the French in Madrid in 1808 disturbed and inspired Goya. He engraved the series of the *Disasters of War* but remained royal painter, portraying the reactionary Ferdinand VII. Finally, in 1824 he joined liberal friends in exile at Bordeaux, where he died.

The Gallery possesses two other portraits by Goya – one of the Duke of Wellington – and also two small pictures, *A Picnic* and a *Scene from a Play*, which show his grasp of reality and fantasy.

DR. PERAL

Dr. Peral is said to have been the financial representative in Paris of the Spanish Government at the end of the 18th century. His appearance does not inspire much confidence; but the confusion of his own country and still more the confusion of Paris at the period may account for something. Goya's ruthless probing of the personality may account for more. In Goya the 18th century's interest in psychology sharpens to a knife point as he peels from his sitters their pretensions to rank or power. He is almost the Stendhal of painters, but his scrutiny of the period in which they both lived is the more merciless. It becomes an ordeal to be portrayed by him: an ordeal which Dr. Peral actually survives rather well as he in turn subjects the spectator to shrewd scrutiny. One great Spanish predecessor stood behind Goya, Velázquez, and Goya recognized his debt. Nothing had made Velázquez's gaze swerve from what he saw; and the marvellous range of the grey tonal harmony of Dr. Peral recalls the low-toned colour schemes of Velázquez. In both painters the colours are broken, diffused, shot through with suggestions of contrast, until they become impossible to define as colours. The paint of Dr. Peral's waistcoat is a subtle silvery colour, almost white in the full light, shadowed to grey at his waist: all framed by the deeper watery-gleaming grey of the coat. This brilliant virtuosity of the brush, in which it is paint not draughtsmanship that suggests the shapes, unites Goya to Gainsborough.

Panel, 37⅜ × 25⅞ (0·950 × 0·657).   Presented by Sir George Donaldson in 1904; earlier recorded in a collection in Paris and at the end of the 19th century acquired by a Spanish collector from the grand-daughter of Dr. Peral in Seville.

Sir Thomas LAWRENCE

(1769–1830)

He was born at Bristol and was an infant prodigy, already drawing likenesses at the age of four or five. In 1787 he entered the Royal Academy Schools but was almost entirely self-taught; the following year he exhibited his first oil portrait. He soon had a great success, becoming A.R.A. in 1791 and R.A. in 1794. He was elected President of the Royal Academy in 1820, and had been knighted in 1815. His brilliant portrait gifts were imaginatively employed all over Europe at the end of the Napoleonic wars when he visited Germany, Austria and Italy, painting the Allied Sovereigns and victorious generals, etc. The resulting portraits are hung in the Waterloo Chamber at Windsor Castle.

QUEEN CHARLOTTE

This portrait was painted in 1789, nearly thirty years before Delacroix's portrait of Baron Schwiter. Yet the two pictures share a great deal, in the actual handling of paint and in the romantic attitude of the painters to their sitters. Lawrence's portrait is of course very early work; only the year before it was painted he had exhibited his first oil portrait at the Royal Academy and his prodigiously successful career had hardly begun. At a later date he was to give his sitters considerably more glamour than he does to the homely figure of Queen Charlotte, but he was to become a flashier painter altogether. The effect here is of a kindly dignity, and the Queen's personality is recognisably that recorded by Fanny Burney who served five rather miserable years as Mistress of the Robes. Though, like her husband, often maligned by contemporaries, the Queen was far from unintelligent and was fond of literature and music. It was to her that the very young Mozart dedicated a group of sonatas, and Queen Charlotte rewarded him with a present of fifty guineas. In the bracelet on the Queen's right wrist is a miniature of George III and in the background Eton College Chapel is seen among the russet autumnal trees. The first sitting given to Lawrence was in late September and the view here – one of the rare pieces of landscape in his work – records the period the picture was begun. His bravura, and yet still careful, handling has been revealed by recent cleaning. The sweep of aquamarine curtain and the crackling lilac paint of the dress are laid on not only with confidence but with intense response to their sensuous effect.

Canvas, 94¼ × 58 (2·395 × 1·47). Bought by the Gallery from Lady Ridley in 1927. Previously in the collection of the Ridley family since its purchase by Sir Matthew White Ridley, 3rd. Bart., in the posthumous Lawrence sale of 18th June 1831. It had been exhibited at the R.A. in 1790.

Joseph Mallord William TURNER
(1775-1851)

He was the son of a barber and was born in Maiden Lane, Covent Garden. Early precocious, he was admitted to the Royal Academy Schools in 1789 and two years later was exhibiting at the Academy itself. In his early years he worked almost exclusively as a water-colourist but he exhibited oil pictures from 1796. In 1799 he became A.R.A. and in 1802 R.A. He travelled abroad a good deal but did not go to Italy until 1819. After his early successes, his increasing interest in subtle effects of light and atmosphere led him to lose public favour. Nowadays, it is probably his latest pictures, oils and water-colours, which are most appreciated. Turner's own character remains mysterious, symbolised in some ways by his strange poem, with its deeply pessimistic title *Fallacies of Hope*, quotations from which accompanied several of his exhibited pictures.

Most of Turner's pictures and drawings were bequeathed to the Nation. The National Collections, shared between the National and Tate Galleries and the British Museum, contain a wide range of his work.

ULYSSES DERIDING POLYPHEMUS

It was perhaps his admiration for Claude that prompted Turner in the first place to take classical subject matter for his paintings. Here the subject derives from Homer – from Book IX of the *Odyssey*—but it is almost Chapman's Homer, working as it worked on the imagination of Keats, that has produced the gorgeous fabric of this atmospheric vision. The blinded, raging Cyclops can just be discerned at the left, a vaporous shape hardly more substantial than the clouds; in the brilliant rays of the rising sun can be made out the horses of the sun; and the escaping Ulysses and his crew are present on the gilded romantic ship. But these touches of the classical story hardly matter, so transmuted has the scene become into a cosmic pageant of the elements. We are travelling in some magic realm which, as so often with Turner at his finest, is compounded largely of sea and sky. It is a glassy, early-morning sea, so bright that the phosphorescent creatures who guide the ship to safety might be no more than the crests of waves caught by the first sunlight. Above, the sky is one of Turner's mighty caverns of atmosphere, an arched perspective of shimmering subtle colour, where night gives place to day in a mauvish haze flecked with rags of molten cloud and reaching a white brilliance in the actual disk of the sun which seems to have abruptly burst on the horizon. The literary ostensible subject perhaps allows Turner the freedom to create equally epic effects, in which the elements echo Ulysses' victory over the Cyclops. The ship glides away from the rocky coast and into the tremendous glow of dawn that floods in a path of light along the water. In place of Constable's facts, Turner exults in dreams. Nature is interpreted in great symphonic poems, of colour not sound, but which yet remind one of Berlioz and Mendelssohn.

Canvas, 52¼ × 80 (1·325 × 2·03). Bequeathed by the painter in 1857; exhibited at the Royal Academy in 1829.

43

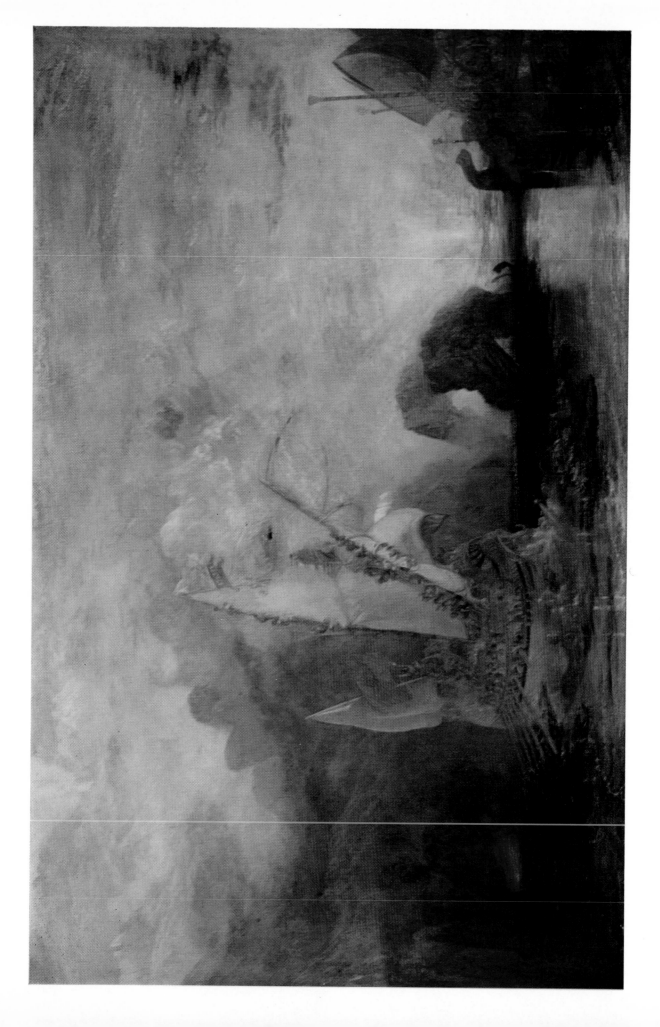

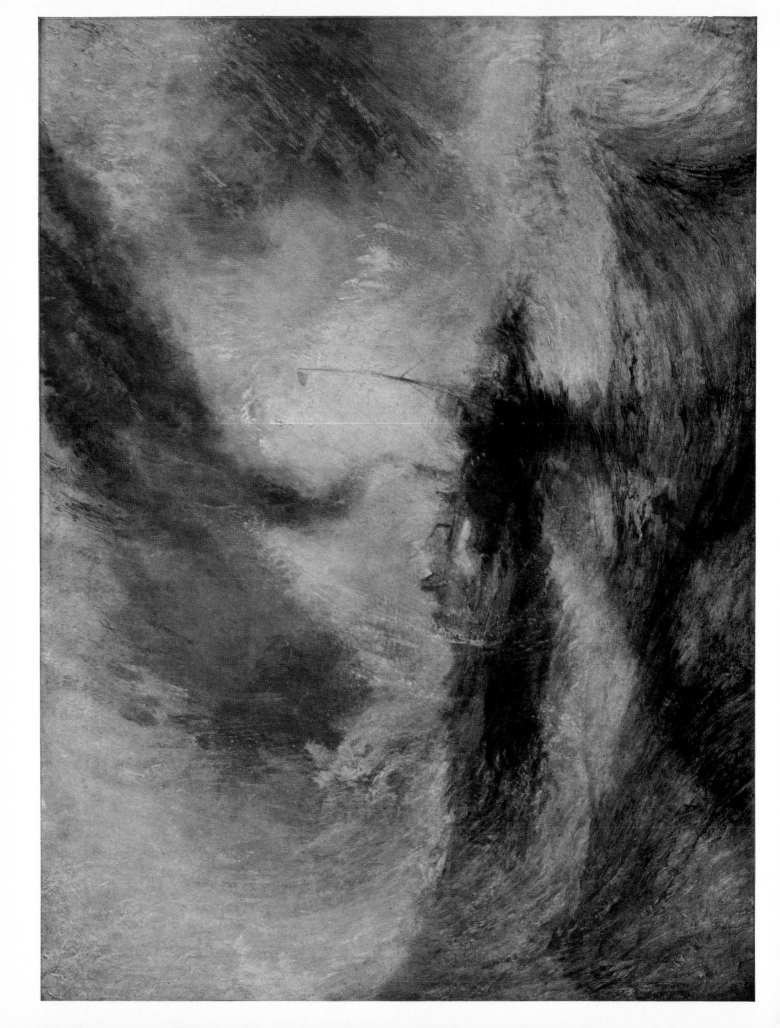

Joseph Mallord William TURNER

(1775-1851)

He was the son of a barber and was born in Maiden Lane, Covent Garden. Early precocious, he was admitted to the Royal Academy Schools in 1789 and two years later was exhibiting at the Academy itself. In his early years he worked almost exclusively as a water-colourist but he exhibited oil pictures from 1796. In 1799 he became A.R.A. and in 1802 R.A. He travelled abroad a good deal but did not go to Italy until 1819. After his early successes, his increasing interest in subtle effects of light and atmosphere led him to lose public favour. Nowadays, it is probably his latest pictures, oils and water-colours, which are most appreciated. Turner's own character remains mysterious, symbolised in some ways by his strange poem, with its deeply pessimistic title *Fallacies of Hope*, quotations from which accompanied several of his exhibited pictures.

Most of Turner's pictures and drawings were bequeathed to the Nation. The National Collections, shared between the National and Tate Galleries and the British Museum, contain a wide range of his work.

A STEAMER IN A SNOWSTORM

Incorrigibly literary, Turner usually sent his pictures to the Royal Academy with titles as long as the captions to jokes in mid-Victorian volumes of *Punch*. The present painting was shown there in 1842, entitled 'Snow Storm – Steamboat off a harbour's mouth making signals in shallow water, and going by the lead'. To this was added a piece of biography, 'The author was in this storm on the night the Ariel left Harwich'. We are thus given all the facts to enable us to appreciate this picture, the origin of which may have been a bad storm at the end of January 1842. Time has made the title largely irrelevant, and it is a question what it has done to the picture. It would not be hard to see it through the spume-cloud of Ruskin's eloquence: a battle of the elements in which a man-made object is their sport. In fact, Ruskin found fault with this particular Turner, remarking in his primly final way 'the sea is . . . not quite right: it is not yeasty *enough* . . .'. And the picture was apparently criticised at the time as being a mass of 'soapsuds and whitewash'. It is quite true that the violent storm witnessed by Turner has lost something of its elemental grandeur in being captured on a canvas of a few feet. Nor were storms at sea a novelty in painting – going back at least as far as Pieter Brueghel. But no one before Turner had attempted to seize the very essence of the sea and to subordinate everything to depiction of scenes where water and sky merge into an atmospheric whole.

Canvas, 36 × 48 (0·915 × 1·22). Bequeathed by Turner to the Nation, the bequest being disputed and settled only in 1856. Exhibited at the R.A. 1842.

John CONSTABLE

(1776-1837)

He was born at East Bergholt in Suffolk and was thus a native of the same county as Gainsborough, whose work he greatly admired. In 1800 he was a student at the Royal Academy Schools in London, but he was largely self-taught and his artistic development was slow. He exhibited first at the Royal Academy in 1802; he became A.R.A. in 1819 and R.A. ten years later. There are some portraits by Constable, but he concentrated on landscape painting and it is his landscapes that have made him famous. During his lifetime he had little popular or critical success in England, but the exhibition of *The Hay-Wain* at the Paris Salon in 1824 had some effect on young French painters, Delacroix (q.v.) among them.

The National Collection, shared between the Tate and National Galleries, contains many pictures by Constable; in addition a fine range of his work is at the Victoria and Albert Museum.

THE CORNFIELD

In the year of Constable's death a body of subscribers presented this picture to the National Gallery where it should represent the painter. Large, elaborately composed, 'not neglected in any part' (as Constable himself had said when sending it to the Royal Academy in 1826), it is the public aspect of an artist who is preferred today in his more private aspect. His instinctive feeling for atmosphere finds its best expression in those sketches which while he lived were too little 'finished' to be suitable for exhibition. But *The Cornfield*, even in its massive elaboration, is part of Constable's high moral seriousness before the spectacle of English landscape; and the landscape itself is the Suffolk countryside of his childhood. The lane led from East Bergholt towards the pathway to Dedham across the meadows; the church in the background, however, apparently never existed. In describing the picture, Constable chose a quotation from Thomson's *Seasons*. He did not select his contemporary Wordsworth (with whom he is so often compared) but a poet entirely of the 18th century: belonging in his childhood as did the first images of East Bergholt and Dedham, with their fields of ripe corn shaken by gusts of autumn wind. This is the reality that mattered to Constable. 'Imagination', he said, 'can never produce works that are to stand by a comparison with realities.' He wanted no enlargement of his experience, never travelled abroad, lived uneventfully. England was his subject, a pastoral England not yet destroyed by the Industrial Revolution. With his immense respect for facts, Constable became the recorder of a rich arable world disappeared for ever.

Canvas, 56¼ × 48 (1·43 × 1·22). Presented in 1837 by a body of subscribers, under the chairmanship of the painter Sir William Beechey, who had bought the picture at Constable's death. Probably exhibited at the Paris Salon in 1827; exhibited at the Royal Academy in 1826.

Jean-Auguste-Dominique INGRES

(1780-1867)

Jean-Auguste-Dominique Ingres was born at Montauban and was trained first under his father. From 1797 he was in Paris working in the studio of Jacques-Louis David. In 1801 he won the *Prix de Rome* but did not go to Italy for another five years. He arrived in Rome in 1806 and remained there until 1820 when he moved to Florence. Not until 1826 did he return to Paris where he had his first great Salon success with the *Vow of Louis XIII*. Ten years later he went back to Rome as director of the French Academy, spending until 1841 there.

The Gallery possesses several pictures by him, both portraits and small subject pictures, but nothing else of comparable importance and size to *Madame Moitessier*.

MADAME MOITESSIER SEATED

Ingres at first declined to paint Madame Moitessier. Then he met her, and agreed. She was to be seated on a sofa with her daughter, Catherine, at her knee, and the first sittings were begun in 1844-45. Many years later the daughter remembered the large cold room where she and her mother posed. But suddenly the '*charmante Catherine*' became for Ingres '*l'insupportable Catherine*' and she was banished from the picture. Ingres had set out to wrestle with the problem of Madame Moitessier alone, and the picture took twelve years to complete. In that time he painted a portrait of Madame Moitessier standing; there was talk of him painting Monsieur Moitessier; Ingres' wife died; he himself was growing old and deaf. The problems raised by this picture remained, and Madame Moitessier – *belle et bonne* as he called her – waited patiently. He changed the colour of her dress, altered her jewellery, begged her to wear a particular bracelet and certain ribbons in her hair. The long love-affair (with the sitter, perhaps, as with the picture) finally resulted in 1856 in this superb late flowering of his genius. Here she sits, incarnation of woman as Ingres conceived woman: not the prisoner of her over heated, over-upholstered, Second Empire environment, but its personification. And she is also a marvel of formal beauty, as is the whole picture in which no detail is trivial or merely pretty. *Le dessin comprend tout excepté la teinte*, Ingres said; that is the controlling force behind this portrait.

Canvas, 47¼ × 36¼ (1·20 × 0·92). Signed and dated 1856. Acquired by the Gallery in 1936 when purchased, through Messrs. Jacques Seligmann, from the descendants of the sitter. Exhibited in the Ingres exhibition at Paris in the year of his death, 1867.

Ferdinand-Victor-Eugène DELACROIX

(1798–1863)

Delacroix was the leading painter of the Romantic Movement in France and was interested also in contemporary English painters. He visited England in 1825, and travelled in Morocco in 1832. Although his first exhibit at the Salon in 1822, the *Barque de Dante*, was well received, his later work was often bitterly attacked and he was placed in artistic opposition to Ingres (q.v.) – tainly his greatest rival. He received several large-scale decorative commissions, of which the finest is probably the late work in a chapel at Saint-Sulpice. He kept a journal which is fascinating not only for its revelation of the artist's intelligence but for its evocation of social life in Paris, seen by a friend of Chopin and George Sand.

The Gallery owns three other pictures by Delacroix, including a typical literary subject-picture, *Ovid among the Scythians* (exhibited at the Salon in 1859).

BARON SCHWITER

Both artist and sitter were still in their twenties when this portrait was painted. The picture has a great deal of youthful romanticism and something of the dandified exuberence of Paris at the period. It is the period of the young Berlioz, and Baron Schwiter might well be the Byronic hero of some symphonic poem by that composer. In fact he was himself a painter of sorts, and also a collector; he owned, as well as some 18th-century French pictures, a few pictures by Tiepolo (an artist Delacroix is said to have admired). The portrait here is very much more successful than the clumsy setting; and even as a portrait it owes part of its effect to the accident of a striking sitter and the dandified restraint of his costume. Part of the landscape background is said to be the work of a certain Paul Huet but, if so, is not a very encouraging example of his talent. And the picture was refused at the Salon of 1827; it remained in Baron Schwiter's possession until his death. In contrast with the hectic baroque of many of his subject pictures, Delacroix's portraits often have a brooding sombreness which Baron Schwiter merely suggests. Delacroix's own self-portrait reveals a character less dreamy and more tortured; and his imagination goaded him on until finally it left him exhausted. Baron Schwiter had the good fortune not to be a great painter, and his imagination probably did not keep him awake at nights.

Canvas, 85¾ × 56½ (2·18 × 1·435). Signed. Bought by the Gallery at the Edgar Degas sale, Paris, 26th March 1918 (lot 24) Probably passed into the collection of Degas not long after the Baron de Schwiter sale at Paris in 1890.

Édouard MANET

(1832–1883)

Édouard Manet studied first under Couture in Paris in the years 1850–56 but was significantly influenced by Goya, Velazquez and other Old Masters, including Hals. He became prominent at the Salon des Refusés in 1863 at which his *Déjeuner sur l'Herbe* was shown and caused a scandal. He was looked on as leader of the Impressionists and they in turn influenced him considerably towards the end of his life, especially in working in the open air.

The Gallery possesses several pictures by him, including fragments of one version of the *Execution of the Emperor Maximilian* and *The Waitress* ('*La Servante des Bocks*').

LA MUSIQUE AUX TUILERIES

Because Manet's pictures created such an outcry in 19th-century Paris, Manet is easily thought of as revolutionary in more than painting. But he did not glory in being rejected by the Salon and execrated by the critics; he wished to be accepted by his period in which he felt very much at home. Society attracted him and he used often to go sketching in the afternoons in the Tuileries where twice a week the band played .The gardens of the palace, then occupied by Napoleon III, were a centre for smart Parisian life of which a microcosm is presented in this picture, which includes many portraits of Manet's friends. Manet himself is at the extreme left. He would lunch at the Café Tortoni and then, usually accompanied by Baudelaire, stroll in the gardens and sketch; from such sketches the picture here was probably assembled. Baudelaire also is included among the crowd, just above the bonnet of the left-hand seated woman in the foreground; eager to find a painter of contemporary life and contemporary costume, he hailed in Manet a taste for *la réalité moderne*. The picture is slight against Manet's later greater work, but it is one of his first pictures of the contemporary scene. Here he creates an *impression* of that life: with its black and ugly clothes (which time has made seem charming), its famous men, its leisurely tempo of existence. As this crowd sit listening to the band, they may be claimed almost as waiting for something: perhaps the birth of Modern Art?

Canvas, 30 × 46½ (0·76 × 1·18). Signed and dated 1862. Acquired by the Gallery through the bequest of Sir Hugh Lane in 1917. It had previously belonged to the firm of Durand-Ruel who had obtained it from the singer, J.-B. Faure, who in turn acquired it from Manet himself. It was twice exhibited in Paris during Manet's lifetime: in 1863 and at the Manet exhibition of 1867.

Paul CÉZANNE

(1839-1906)

He was born at Aix-en-Provence and this environment was to play a significant part in his art. In 1861, having abandoned study of the law, he went to Paris where he met Camille Pissarro; he exhibited at the first Impressionist exhibition of 1874, but his aims were quite different from those of the Impressionists, being directed to exploration of form as well as colour. After the death of his father in 1886 he lived in retirement near Aix at a house called Jas de Bouffan. He painted mainly landscapes and still life; there are a few portraits, including some self-portraits.

The National Collection, shared between the Tate and National Gallery, contains several paintings by Cézanne; at Trafalgar Square, in addition to *Les Grandes Baigneuses*, there are portraits and landscapes by him.

LES GRANDES BAIGNEUSES

Cézanne once said that he wanted to make of Impressionism something solid and durable: 'like the art of the museums'. It is in the light of this aim that one can consider *Les Grandes Baigneuses*, one version of three large canvases on this theme which occupied the painter intermittently during the last ten years or so of his life. It takes as its subject the Renaissance concept of bodies out in the open air – not illustrating any particular story but concerned with nature and natural settings. Cézanne was a constant visitor to the Louvre, and his *Grandes Baigneuses* canvases are to some extent modern interpretations of the famous picture in the Louvre *Le Concert Champêtre* which was then thought to be by Giorgione. That picture was revolutionary in the early years of the sixteenth century at Venice. Cézanne's style is equally a revolution, a deliberate departure first from the standard of academic realism and then from the visual truths of Impressionism. In some senses the picture is already an abstract of nature: though so firmly based on the sensuous effects of sunlight on flesh in a setting of trees and grass, it has recreated their poetry in elemental forms, bold blocks of bodies which take on an increasing sense of volume amid the blue-green palpitating atmosphere which surrounds them. Nature remains the spur to these sensations which – rather like heat dazzle – are emitted by the picture. Paint has been laid on so thickly that it is almost like enamel, but translucent, molten enamel – deep green and intense, inky blue. It is a passionate expression of Cézanne's attachment to things seen and his pursuit of a personal vision. In one way *Les Grandes Baigneuses* closes a tradition extending back to Giotto; in another it opens the path towards the achievements of painting in the twentieth century.

Canvas, 50⅛ × 77⅜ (1·272 × 1·961). Acquired by the Gallery in 1964, with assistance from the Max Rayne Foundation and a Supplementary Grant. Previously in the Pellerin-Lecomte collection, Paris, having been acquired by Auguste Pellerin and bequeathed in 1929 to his daughter Madame Lecomte.

Claude-Oscar MONET

(1840–1926)

He was born in Paris but went as a child to Le Havre. Under the influence of Boudin, whom he met there, he became a landscape painter. After doing a period of conscription he returned to Paris where he was to become the leading member of the group of Impressionist painters, meeting Sisley, Renoir, Manet, etc. It was his picture, exhibited in 1874 – entitled 'An Impression' – which led to the derisive term Impressionism being given to the whole movement, now recognized as a major force in modern painting. Monet concentrated in his late years on painting series of pictures centred on a single subject – Poplar trees, Haystacks, Rouen Cathedral. The most famous of all are the series, of which there is more than one, concerned with *Nymphéas* (Water-lilies) which occupied him as a theme for as long as he could paint.

In the National Collection, divided between the National and Tate Galleries, are seven other pictures by Monet, including *Le Bassin aux Nymphéas* (National Gallery) which is dated 1899 and is among Monet's earliest treatments of the theme.

WATER LILIES

As soon as Monet bought his house at Giverny in 1890 he began to make a water-lily garden, over which he built a Japanese-style bridge. The pool and bridge formed the subject of his first views, seen from a normal viewpoint. Then Monet altered the effect, to give the spectator a view – perhaps originally suggested by standing on the bridge – of looking down into the water, with the lilies floating amid reflections on its surface. From that came the concept of a whole inter-linked series of long canvases, to give the sense of a sea washing limitlessly around the spectator. Urged on by his friend, the statesman Clemenceau, Monet had a new studio built on a large scale, to accommodate the big canvases he planned for the new series. The studio was not completed until 1916. In the following year Clemenceau accepted a group of *Nymphéas* from Monet as a gift to the State, but these were still on a comparatively small scale. Finally, nineteen large canvases – on a scale of over six feet high and almost fourteen feet wide – were installed in the Orangerie of the Tuileries Gardens. The present picture is like these in scale but even more freely painted. Composition in the accepted sense has been banished; and subject matter is no longer important – indeed, one might not immediately realise the subject. Instead, in an almost musical way, the picture evokes a mood. A few patches of bright colour float on the shimmering canvas – not a surface but a depth. The spectator is encouraged to sink his personality in this yellow nirvana in which objects have ceased to exist and everything is fused into one peaceful whole.

Canvas, 79–168 (2·0 × 4·27). Posthumous stamp: *Claude Monet*. Bought from the Galerie Beyeler, Bâle, with a Special Grant, 1963. Exhibited earlier in Paris in 1956, when owned by Katia Granof.